THE TRACES OF GOD

International Standard Book Number: 0-936384-03-4
Library of Congress Catalog Number: 80-51570

©1981 by Cowley Publications
Published in the United States of America by Cowley Publications

Printed by Shea Brothers, Inc.
Designed by James Madden, SSJE

THE
TRACES
OF GOD

IN A FREQUENTLY HOSTILE WORLD

Diogenes Allen

COWLEY

for
Joseph and Mary Billing

ACKNOWLEDGMENTS

My debt to various writers is acknowledged at appropriate points in this book, but I wish to make one particular acknowledgement here. The route of desire, the route of beauty, and the three levels of human need are major themes in the work of Simone Weil. The ultimate source of these is Plato; Weil, however, did not limit herself to what Plato said, but used his ideas freely. I have not limited myself, in turn, to what either Weil or Plato said, but have developed ideas in my own way. The soundness or unsoundness of what I say here in regard to these matters will have to be judged on its own merits, despite the immense profit I have derived from both writers.

I have been very fortunate in my editors with everything I have written before, but have been exceptionally well served on this occasion. Hugh T. Kerr, editor of *Theology Today* for over three decades, endured with patience and good grace my attempts to deal with the theme of suffering at the hands of nature, until a much better piece of work resulted. Although chapter four is the only part of the manuscript he saw, his response affected large parts of the whole.

Cynthia Bell, editor of Cowley Publications, supplied me with the most helpfully interpreted readers' reports I have ever had, as well as many thoughtful and intelligent observations of her own. She has shown in every way that the making of books can once again be a pleasure.

Chapter four of this book, "Suffering at the Hands of Nature," has appeared in slightly different form in the July 1980 issue of *Theology Today*. Some material from this same chapter forms part of an article directed to a philosophical audience; entitled "Natural Evil and the Love of God," it will appear in a forthcoming issue of *Religious Studies,* Cambridge University Press.

Diogenes Allen

Princeton Theological Seminary
July, 1980

CONTENTS

INTRODUCTION

THE INTERSECTION OF TWO REALMS

Christianity claims that life can be wonderful, and we all certainly want it to be. Yet so often it isn't. Consider these fragments of an autobiographical statement by a young man.

> I left the Church because it no longer seemed relevant to my problems. I had already been saved and I was looking for some help in living in the world before it was time to go to heaven. I did not forsake my conversion experience. . . .
>
> In college my fragile faith bit the dust.
>
> Working at a truck line loading freight crushed the vision of Camelot.

There are several things here that more or less fit many of us: lack of a satisfactory method for coping with life, not enough help from the church, a faith that is unable to withstand the corrosive acid of intellectual examination, a belief in personal happiness that evaporates when it encounters the harsh realities of life.

The world frustrates many of our deepest longings, and is frequently even hostile, yet these facts do not contradict the truth of Christianity. The heart of Christianity is the living God who brings us joy and who can be present to us in the midst of dissatisfaction, frustration, and even the severest sufferings. The harsh realities of life, the bumps and bruises we endure, need not wipe out the lovely side of life and make belief in our personal happiness impossible. These harsh realities do destroy sentimentality, including religious sentimentality. They do not destroy the foundation of all reality, the one who is above all that we can see, measure, and weigh.

Although God is beyond the world, he makes contact with us in and through the world he created, and "touches" both the world and us at many points. My intention is to describe the various ways we can be aware of this presence and experience it. For God comes to us not in spite of our dissatisfaction with our daily lives, but precisely because of it — we can find his love not only in what is lovely, pleasant, and good, but also in what is upsetting, frightening, and painful. God is the ruler of all, so we can find his love even in and through our worst suffering. In all that is negative, something can be found that is positive and creative, that can make us aware of the hidden glory in what we so often take for granted. It is not by turning our backs on the harsh realities of life that we can find help in our daily lives, but by facing them, so that we do not merely keep our dreams of personal happiness alive but learn what happiness really is.

But it is not only the frustrations and hard knocks of life which destroy our dreams of personal happiness and make God seem remote. Part of our difficulty in knowing the joy of his presence is that we are unable to form a picture of God himself. Perhaps this is why extraordinary phenomena, such as miraculous healings and speaking in tongues, are sometimes emphasized instead of God's presence in ordinary and daily life. The unusual and inexplicable do seem to confirm our belief in the reality of him whom we otherwise cannot imagine. But even though we cannot form a photographic image of God, we can conceive of him with the help of some ideas, ideas that help open us to his reality so that we may know his presence.

They may also enable us to recognize that he has probably already visited us more often than we have realized.

Let me show how this works, and how abstract ideas can make something accessible to our own experience. Most of us have an *idea* of how football is played, and have had more than once the experience of deep anguish when, at a crucial point in the game, a long pass just trickles off the fingertips of the receiver. But if we do not understand football at all, or have little idea of the game, we could see exactly the same thing and feel nothing but wonder at the groans of the crowd.

Our emotions and intellect are not separate. Nothing could be more emotional than the anguished disappointment felt by the football fans in this example, but it is felt only because they understand what the event is — an incomplete pass at a crucial moment. Although the intellect is not to the fore at the time anguish is felt, nonetheless the emotion is possible only because the mind understands what is taking place. At an earlier time, when the rules of football were learned, the intellect took first place and the emotions were not so prominent, though not utterly absent. So there is always an interaction between the mind and the emotions, between the abstract and the concrete, between ideas and the experience which these ideas help to identify. Without experience, our ideas are empty; without ideas, we cannot put a name to whatever it is with which we are in touch. So throughout this book I shall from time to time present ideas, but will be concerned above all with what is concrete: the contact between God and us. The ideas do not *create* the experience, but they enable us to recognize God's presence and to be aware of this contact when it occurs.

One of the ideas which can help us understand the presence of God combines two elements. First, God is different from all that is earthly, and therefore he is in a dimension that is utterly inaccessible to us; second, we are able to have contact with him. Now these two aspects of a single idea seem to be contradictory, but we can come to understand how this is possible by an analogy. Imagine a flat surface, which a geometer would call a plane, and assume that everything we can experience is on that plane — the human plane, so to speak. Now if there is a divine reality, we could have no experience of it unless its plane touched or intersected our own. In that case most of it would still not be on our plane, but only that small part of it which crossed the human plane; most of the divine reality would remain outside and be still unknown. The point of intersection would occupy only a small part of the human plane, so most of human experience would not have any apparent contact with divine reality.

This idea of intersecting planes may help us to conceive of God as a reality who is both beyond us and who also reaches us, and who therefore is partially known by us. It is an especially useful idea because it can also show us why faith in the reality of God is so easily eroded by the present intellectual climate in which we live, where faith in God seems to be a worn-out belief unable to sustain itself. Since God is unknowable and unimaginable unless he crosses the plane of human experience, whatever we identify as the presence of God is always something on the human plane. Just because it *is* on the human plane, we can always claim that the phenomenon is "natural" — unless it is extraordinary and inexplicable, like the miracles I spoke of earlier. Unless there is something unusual about such an event, there is nothing to aid our recognition of the divine reality crossing our plane. Alternatively, if the experience is unusual or bizarre, it can still easily be dismissed. For example, let us say that the divine enters the human realm in the form of a voice which is heard by someone, or a vision seen. If we do not happen to experience these ourselves, then we can always reject the reality of the divine plane. We neither heard the voice nor saw the vision, and the experiences of others can always be explained away as psychological abnormalities. Think of people in mental institutions who describe religious experiences very similar to those reported both in the Bible and by great religious leaders such as George Fox, the founder of the Society of Friends.[1]

If the alleged divine phenomena are events, such as the parting of the Red Sea in the book of Exodus, a similar difficulty arises. We must depend on historical evidence to verify the alleged events. The events recorded in the Bible were written down long before modern standards of reportage had developed, so it is extremely difficult for historians today to specify what in ancient stories is history, and what is myth or legend. Miracles, such as the Red Sea parting at just the right moment during the pursuit of the Jews by the Egyptians, are certainly not impossible, but historians have such insufficient data that they find it hard to establish the degree of probability, and thus give some basis for belief that divine reality had in fact intersected the human plane. So it is always possible to dismiss miraculous events found in the Bible as reports of ancient people who were less critically minded than we are today.

The most important intersection of the two realms, and that which gives us the most difficulty, is the life of Jesus Christ, the incarnation of the Word of God. According to Christian belief, Jesus is thoroughly human. Because of this, people have had difficulty specifying what it is about him that makes him divine as well, and how we can conceive of him as both fully human and divine at the same time. The idea of two intersecting planes is very useful here. The place of intersection of two planes is a straight line, and that straight line is simultaneously part of, and on, *both* planes. Yet it is of itself a single line. The Word of God is more than what is merely visible and present to us when it becomes incarnate, more than the single line of intersection. Nonetheless it is the Word of God that is incarnate and present in the world in Jesus Christ; the Word of God *is* the single line.

This illustration of intersecting planes also shows why it is so easy to deny Jesus' divinity. Since all we have before us is a single line of the human plane, we must go on to specify what it is about Jesus that allows us to say that he extends far beyond what we can see before us into the invisible, divine realm, and exists simultaneously on two planes. If whatever we can point to on the human plane is not *unique* to Jesus, then it can always be said that we have no basis for claiming that he is a different kind of reality. If, on the other hand, what we point to is unusual, such as Jesus' power to perform miracles, we can be challenged from two different sides. The miracles can be denied as mere legend, or else Jesus' power to perform miracles may be conceded without conceding his divinity, since other people in ancient times were reported to have this power and they were not divine.

I shall examine this more fully later on, but for now I can say that to call Jesus the incarnation of the Word of God is as open to question as all lesser claims of the presence of the divine in the human realm. Those who do not believe in a divine reality can always interpret the place of intersection — the sole point of our contact with the divine — as a point that is merely on the human plane, and not as one on the divine plane as well. Because every point of intersection is in the world, we can always claim that it is *of* this world as well. No wonder that young man, with whose autobiographical statement we began, found his fragile faith eroded at university. Because the very place where God makes himself available is on the human plane, it is relatively easy to dismiss every revelation of God. We can remain oblivious to the presence of another dimension on the human plane by dismissing everything believers claim either as the result of superstition and abnormality, when it is about unusual or bizarre events or experience, or by refusing to see that ordinary "natural" events can be at the same time revelatory.

One reason that there is such a strong tendency today to reduce everything to a single plane is the loss of a sense of mystery in the modern world. This process of demystification began more than three hundred years ago, and much of this tendency is valuable and sound. We do have, on the whole, a better understanding of history and of historical study, and of the natural sciences, especially astronomy, biology, physics, and chemistry. A great deal of superstition has been exposed and removed from our investigations of the universe and its workings. It is my desire, however, to seek to reintroduce a sense of mystery into our world, though not by drawing on bizarre experiences, or fringe phenomena such as ESP, or by merely identifying the mysterious with the unusual. Mystery can be present in something as simple and apparently prosaic as forgiving someone, or seem as ordinary as the ability to be free of the burden of envy. Although these acts are in one sense perfectly "ordinary," they are not, as we shall see, reducible to the human plane. Although the human plane is where such acts occur, they partake simultaneously of another dimension.

In addition, mystery is not to be identifed simply with the unknown. We often use the word that way when we say, for example, that the cause of a disease is still a "mystery." But God is a mystery that is known; not fully known, of course, but known at those points where he intersects our human plane. Even where he intersects our world, the full significance and meaning of what is there is not apparent to us because it is connected to a dimension beyond our view. So God remains a mystery even at those very places where he has revealed himself by crossing into our world. If we become open to the presence of another reality in but not of the world, we shall begin to find that he crosses our plane in many places. In time we can even come to realize that not only does he touch us here and there, but that the entire human plane is in contact with the divine reality in which we live and move and have our being.

This book is an exploration of some of the places where God touches our lives and makes himself known. In my earlier book, *Between Two Worlds,* a guide to the spiritual life was given for those who are beginning to be religious, and I said there was more than one way to describe the Christian pilgrimage. This time I am considering the path that leads through adversity, and will try to show that our sufferings, however frustrating, can be put to good use. Through adversity we can begin to discover God's presence, either for the first time or in new and fresh ways, and to receive his help. It is not pleasant to think about adversity — but if we refuse, not only do we fail to recognize those points where God is present, but we needlessly go without his help. He meets us in the midst of our adversity. The divine love, which became incarnate as Jesus Christ, endured the same adversities as we endure.

The pilgrimage I am going to describe has three main stages, each forming a major division of this book. First, there is our preparation. We must be *prepared* in order to recognize another dimension in our world — a divine one. It does not require any special talent or esoteric technique to do this; the common desire to be happy is where we start. Our preparation consists in facing the fact that we cannot find the happiness we want from anything of this world, a fact realized even by those who have had the most outwardly successful of lives. It was Leonardo da Vinci, a man of peerless talent and achievement, who wrote, "Why am I so unhappy?"

In the second stage the problem of our response to divine love arises, once we have come to acknowledge this love. Then we find ourselves subject to opposing forces, pulled both toward and away from our commitment to Jesus Christ. Our initial attraction to Christ can be counteracted by an opposite pull, our despair at human suffering. Disease, random accidents, storms, and human cruelty pull us away from our faith in a divine realm of love, and our commitment to Christ as its incarnation. An examination of human suffering will, however, give us a deeper knowledge of God's love and may enable us to yield ourselves to it. The third stage of this journey has to do with our behavior. Divine love is active: it creates, redeems, and elevates. If divine love is known and received, we come to share in this activity, and I will examine the kinds of activity divine love inspires in those who receive it.

PART ONE

OUR PREPARATION

Nothing is so insufferable to man as to be completely at rest, without passions, without business, without diversions, without study. He then feels his nothingness, his forlornness, his insufficiency, his dependence, his weakness, his emptiness.

Pascal, *Pensées*

CHAPTER ONE

THE ROUTE OF DESIRE

There are many routes which lead to an encounter with the divine realm and to a knowledge of God's presence, and nearly all of these involve facing the harsh and painful realities of life. Naturally we seek to avoid what is painful and unpleasant, and to alleviate suffering. But we should not refuse to think about it, for we will then miss an opportunity to discover the redemptive presence of God. The kind of suffering I will talk about in this chapter is the least intense of all; it is also the most common, and the most difficult to ignore completely. This is the suffering that comes with the search for a satisfying and rewarding life — an inescapable human desire, and one that Christianity both heartily endorses and promises to satisfy. But this desire for a happy life encounters problems and frustrations which lead all too often to a dissatisfaction with our lives. This is not an accident, for it can be one of the ways God leads us to himself and to a genuinely full life.

I will begin with this route because its starting point, the desire for happiness, is common to us all. Besides, it is this very desire for fullness of life, and the dissatisfaction with what we have made of our lives, which can prepare us for a recognition of the greatest intersection of the divine realm with our own — the incarnation of God in Jesus Christ. This recognition can occur precisely because of what we learn from our pursuit of happiness.

I

We discover the reality of a divine realm by what seems at first to be a paradox, for this discovery is brought about by a refusal. We discover a divine love or presence *initially* by refusing to give ourselves to anything, by withholding ourselves from any source of happiness that we can see or imagine. As human beings we are a mass of wants and desires. We seek things, consume them to satisfy our desires, and no matter how much we get or whatever it is that we get, sooner or later we want more, or we want something else. We never seem to be satisfied with what we possess or achieve; we are restless and crave what is novel.

As Plato puts it, we are like leaky vessels. It is as though we were containers into which we keep pouring things, but we never get filled up because there is a hole in each container and something is always leaking out. So we spend our lives trying to attain fullness, satisfaction, and completeness, and yet we never do. We go on thinking that if only we had just a bit more, then we would be satisfied; if we had something else, then our potential would be realized, our happiness assured, and our fulfillment achieved. We spend our lives seeking to satisfy our never-ending desires, our "loves," as they are called in ancient Greek philosophy. But we never seek God. In fact, we cannot at first seek God; initially, we have no idea of what it is that we are seeking. God is unlike anything of this world, unlike anything that we can imagine.

Not only do we lack an idea of him so that we could seek him if we wished, we have at first no desire for him. Our desires are for things we can *imagine,* and they push us on and on relentlessly from one thing to another, seeking in one place after another to satisfy that hunger for fullness. Some people consume everything in sight; others arrange their lives more prudently so as to gain the maximum of satisfaction, and exercise their imagination on goals they would love to attain. All this holds us firmly fixed to the ground as powerfully as the force of gravity holds our bodies to the earth. We love this world and everything in it that promises to give us fullness of life.

We cannot move an inch toward God; if we are to know him, it will have to be through his coming to us. Those who know God, know that he does come, and travels the infinite distance between himself and the human plane. But his coming to our plane does not of itself do any good. He must be able to enter into us and awaken love in us for himself, for God is love and love can be known only by love. We cannot know him until we love him, until we desire him. Otherwise his presence is like the rain that beats on a roof, that runs off and does not penetrate.

How then can God enter, and how can we come to desire him? Where can we find that one desire for God, that desire which would respond to his love, that one desire that can so master all our other desires for the things of this world that we would indeed seek first the kingdom, and leave the rest subordinate to it? It is not a desire we have. We as creatures consist of nothing but desires which bind us to the earth, thinking as we do that we can determine our own happiness. It is for this reason that love for God begins not with the desire for God, and not with seeking God, but by withholding ourselves from all other things. It begins with our refusal to give our love to anything of this world, our decision to hold back, to renounce, because we realize that there is nothing in this world that can fully satisfy us.

This is a realization that hurts. It hurts because we come to recognize that at our core there is an emptiness, or a void, or a hollow, which nothing can fill. Try as we may, all we can do is to keep it temporarily from our attention, and hold this realization in check for a short while; nothing in the world can fill this void. There is a hole which is part of our very substance, and whatever we put into ourselves drains away, and on and on we crave.

Anyone can see this; it does not take genius. Anyone can see it after thinking about it for fifteen minutes. What *is* hard is to hold onto this realization, to hold to it and refuse to give it up. What is hard is to *attend* to it. To withhold oneself from the world, and refuse to give it one's love, is to eat and drink, work and save, laugh and cry, fail and achieve, and know through it all that fullness of life cannot be attained. To refuse is to know this painful truth and, by the act of holding on to it, to know it as more than a mere idea. In this way its truth increasingly becomes an ingredient of every moment of our awareness, because we live with the hollow or void at the center of ourselves exposed. Naturally we do not like this. To be hungry for life, and to admit that there is no proper food, is to suffer and know that there is no relief. That is why we let all sorts of things rush in to fill that painful emptiness, and will do almost anything except let ourselves feel, know, and live with the fact that we are creatures who crave and crave, and there is nothing of this world to fill us. It is at this time that God comes. If we have withheld ourselves, if we have acted so as to leave the void exposed, then and only then does God have access. There is room in us for his presence.

As the psalmist writes, "Be still, and know that I am God" (Ps. 46:10). This "stillness" can be the realization that there is no place to which we can move that gives us fullness. It is to stand still because finally there is no place to go — no matter how "active" we are. In all our actions there is a lack of motion at the core of our person, an emptiness left uncovered. If that emptiness is endured, then God does come. He comes in secret and plants a seed: the seed of his kingdom, the seed of his rule, the seed of his presence, his very own Spirit. He comes in secret not only because we cannot perceive his presence with our senses, but also because the seed is very small, like the tiny mustard seed of Christ's parable. It must have time to grow. For months, or even years, after the seed has been planted we may remain with our feeling of emptiness unabated. Everything may look the same as before. We must continue to endure emptiness until the seed has grown big enough for us to feel its presence.

So there are two stages to our preparation here, two actions in which we must acquiesce. First, we must make an act of renunciation and thus allow God's gracious presence; secondly, we must endure with patience the period of time when the seed is growing but has not achieved sufficient growth to be felt. The first stage is easier than the second. We may well have learned that we cannot find a satisfactory life for ourselves. But the seed that may have secretly been planted may be expelled simply through our unwillingness to go on living with the sense that life contains no possibility of fullness. Once again we may return to our habit of consuming — be it goods, experiences, or other people — as if fullness could be found there, and seek to realize our ambitions as heedlessly as before. We may even try out the various therapies widely heralded as routes to happiness, or try to find out what is wrong by getting psychiatric help. But Freud himself said that the purpose of psychoanalysis is to enable people who are neurotically unhappy to become normally unhappy. There is a "normal" unhappiness, just as there is a "normal" emptiness. Goods, recognition, people, and psychology can all be used to keep that emptiness at bay. But this use of the world not only prevents God from reaching us, it can even serve to expel the seed which he may already have planted. What is asked of us is to be still — that is what we are to do.

If we continue to endure the truth of what we are — leaky vessels, with no hope of fullness from this world — we are turned in God's direction whether we know it or not. Sooner or later we begin to experience the presence of love within ourselves. One of the fruits of the seed of God's presence in us is a desire for something beyond this world, where before there was only a need. Our former desires were for things that could be sought in earthly activities and achievements; now a desire is present for that which is not earthly. A kind of love has come which was not sought before, one hardly even conceivable. Now there is a desire for *that* love — a love for that love. It is a desire that the world did not give us, but that arose precisely because of a turning from this world and all that we can imagine.

I am describing this love when it has reached a very full and mature state. For most people, in its beginnings, this love only flickers gently now and again, and may be barely recognizable. Nonetheless in every case a love is experienced, and that alone is able to assuage the emptiness at the core of ourselves. It alone gives nourishment for a hunger this world cannot feed.

II

In the *Introduction* I explained how easy it is to reduce what is not of this world to the human plane, because when the divine realm intersects our own it is only on the human plane. The way to show the incorrectness of reducing everything to our plane is to make a closer examination of some of the alleged points of intersection, although not everyone who makes this examination will be able to understand or perceive them accurately. Some things cannot be perceived properly unless we perform some actions. The one act I have described so far — refusing the world — enables us to discover the divine realm, and without performing this action we cannot know a loving presence. Those who have never refused the world are familiar with the word "love," and indeed may have experienced love of many kinds, and may therefore think that they know all kinds. So it might be difficult to see why the experience of love should be thought to be the discovery of a divine realm, rather than a human experience and a human phenomenon.

Those who have endured the void know that they have encountered a distinctive hunger, or emptiness; nothing earthly satisfies it. When they find that this hunger is being fed, they also find that the love they experience is peculiarly distinctive. We, looking at this from the outside, may have difficulty recognizing the distinctive quality of this love simply because the word "love" lacks concision in English. In English we are left with only one word to refer to many different kinds of love, all with the common denominator of joyousness. New Testament writers could distinguish between *agape* and *philia,* for example, and in St. Paul's famous chapter on love in I Corinthians *agape* is used to describe the divine love working in human beings — a term translated by the King James Version as "charity." It is a pity we have lost that designation which is at once more explicit and more subtle than our "love," which has to make do for friendship, passion, divine love, maternal love, and so on.

When we come to describe the characteristics of this love more fully, it will become clear that it is distinctive. This distinctiveness is only to be expected, since the hunger this love feeds is not a hunger for anything earthly. Because this love is not only distinctive, but arises precisely when we turn from the world, those who experience it have very good reason to resist all attempts to reduce it to something of this world.

Throughout this book such resistance will be characteristic of my approach. I will describe the ideas and the actions that open us to a divine presence, as well as the distinctive characteristics of this love and goodness. Merely to do this should be enough to prevent an easy and wholesale reduction by secular minds, forcing us to be more thoughtful and perhaps to recognize at least the possibility of the reality of something beyond this world. Activity is the key, for only through carrying out certain acts can we be convinced of the reality of another realm. So here I want to highlight only one point: the need for action. Mere ideas are not enough to help us recognize and receive that divine presence which comes to us in so many ways. Ideas are necessary, but it is just as necessary to *use* them. Our actions must carry out our ideas. We must do something — in this case, we must refuse the world and endure the emptiness that is at our core. There are other actions that are needed and I will describe them. But here I am stressing that it is the failure to perform certain actions which allows us to reduce all reports and claims of encounters with a divine realm to one plane, and the same failure that keeps us from encountering the divine realm for ourselves.

CHAPTER TWO

THE ROUTE OF HUMILITY

The act of forsaking the world, of withholding from it our love, allows us to receive a divine seed. With this we have gone a little further on our way toward that recognition of the presence, the "traces," of God on the human plane, in whatever place these traces are to be found. At this stage, however, a further action is necessary, and a further renunciation. It is not enough to withhold our devotion from the things of this world, for we must also withhold our use of force, of coercion, and of power. We need not only to refuse the world, insofar as it contains what could give us fullness of life, but also to refuse the use of force as a means of obtaining this fullness.

To put it another way, in order to learn to recognize God's presence on the human plane we must learn to look at the right place. The point at which the life of God intersects our own is not to be found in the realm of power, but in the realm of goodness; not in deeds of force, but in acts of humility. It is easy enough to confuse the two, as when we speak of a powerful human being as "godlike," and mistake divine power for human coercion. So we must shift our attention from the category of power to the category of goodness. Again, this is not an idea to be mulled over and entertained, but an action to be performed.

Not only must we renounce the use of power as a means to fullness of life, we must also be willing to suffer the consequences of its exercise on ourselves. There is a legitimate use of power. What is to be renounced is its *unjust* use as a way to fullness of life, for only then can we notice whatever it is on the human plane that gives access to a divine realm. Only in this way do we encounter a distinctive kind of goodness, invulnerable and indestructible. So now I would like to give an example of what it actually is to renounce the use of force, and how this renunciation can lead to the experience of an indestructible goodness.

I

The example I am using is taken from a radio play by Friedrich Dürrenmatt, a Swiss author, who shortly after the Second World War became one of Europe's best-known writers. Only some of his plays and novels have been translated into English, but several of the plays have been staged in America and he is frequently read in college courses. Like his predecessor Bertolt Brecht, Dürrenmatt focuses on man's inhumanity to man, and also makes the same extensive use of irony. Unlike Brecht, however, whose humor is frequently bitter, Dürrenmatt's is usually good-natured and even light-hearted, so that the most grim portrayal of evil does not sap our hope and courage.

The radio play is called, "Nocturnal Conversation with a Despised Person," and was written in 1951.[2] The setting is somewhere behind the Iron Curtain. A writer, who has spent his entire life protesting against the regime in the name of human freedom and decency, has been forced to live in isolation because people were afraid to associate with him. But he knows that sooner or later someone will be sent to him, if only to arrest him, and hopes to be able to explain to this person — for the last time — what it is he has been struggling for. But the person who comes to his apartment in the dead of night is the public executioner, with orders to slit his throat.

The writer is overwhelmed with disgust, and pours bitter scorn on this massive man who kills on command, and who will even draw a state pension for it. To talk with such a person about freedom and human decency is pointless. He is merely a brutal instrument, a mindless force.

The executioner calmly accepts this reproach. He acknowledges that he knows nothing about freedom. Fifty years ago he committed a crime and, in exchange for his own life, became the public executioner. All these years he has lived in prison. Only recently has he been allowed out at night when he has a special job to perform, such as this one.

The writer is stirred by pity. As a writer, too, he is curious. So he asks, "What is important to an executioner?"

"The way a person dies, Sir," the executioner replies (p. 99). And so a conversation begins in which the executioner describes, on the basis of his vast experience, the different ways in which people die.

At first, the executioner says, he did not notice any difference at all. He was at that time little more than a raw youth, with no discernment, and it seemed to him that to lose one's life was everything; outside of that, nothing mattered. So the executioner assumed it was perfectly natural that a scoundrel should resist him as violently as he could, for he understood that sort of person — indeed, he was one himself. There was crime in their actions and justice in his executions, so everything added up, with nothing left over: "They died a healthy death" (p. 101).

But it soon became clear to him that there were some who died differently, who made "magnificent speeches on freedom and justice, attacked tyranny, so that one felt cold shivers running down the spine." These wanted to show their indifference to death. But "here, too, the calculation was clear and simple: it was war between them and me. They died with anger and scorn, and I struck them in anger; in my opinion, justice lay with both of us. They died an imposing death." (p. 101)

The writer replies that he, too, admires such deaths, and hopes that in his own day there may be many such witnesses to freedom and justice. But the executioner tells him that such witness is no longer possible, because the State holds public trials only when that suits its interests; on those occasions, the condemned person is a broken man. He dies as an animal — indifferent, without defiance or resistance. This sort of death does not make sense, the executioner complains, and people should not accept their deaths with such passivity. Unfortunately people have always died this way, even in the old days before the Revolution. The executioner goes on to say, however, that he has found there is another way to die, even in these times. It is to die humbly.

This statement provokes a violent protest on the part of the writer, who argues that one should protest against the crimes committed against humanity with one's last breath. He is furious at the outrage about to be committed against him. In his own house, surrounded by his books — monuments to human nobility — he is to be killed without a public charge, trial, defense, or even the pronouncement of a sentence. Indeed, he is to die without a clergyman — something even a criminal used to have — and he is told to die humbly! Instead, he will resist. The writer turns to the open window and screams aloud that he is being slaughtered like an animal. "Come and see what sort of State we live in today!" (p. 104)

No one comes. Even though the writer shouts again and again not a sound is heard on the streets, although it is almost dawn, nor is a footstep to be heard in the apartment building. He is defeated. Even worse, he feels like a fool for having fought against the might of the State with his puny intellectual weapons, "like a Don Quixote, who advanced against evil with good prose" (p. 105). Now he wants to yield himself to the executioner's knife without further struggle, like a man who is worn-out and broken. But the executioner tells him he ought not to die this way. There is another way to die, and that is to die as one of the humble; this is what he must do.

But what does it mean to die humbly? the writer asks.

> Nothing is as difficult to understand as humility, Sir. It takes a long time for a person to recognize it. At first I used always to despise it, until I recognized that it is the great master of death. If one dies as indifferently as an animal, then he yields himself to me and lets me strike him without defending himself. Humility is utterly different. It is not resignation because of exhaustion. Then I thought, "It is the result of deep anxiety." But it is precisely the humble who have no anxiety. Finally I believed that I had found out: the humble were the criminals who accepted their deaths as a punishment.

Now, that sort of death made sense to the executioner. A crime is cancelled out by its punishment, so to speak, with nothing left in the balance. But, he goes on to say,

> the only remarkable thing is that innocent people also died that way, people of whom I knew for certain that my blows fell upon unfairly. . . . The humility of the criminal was clear to me, but that an innocent person could also die that way, I didn't grasp. And they even died just as if no crime were being committed on them and as if they underwent their death justly. I was afraid for a long time when I had to strike and, candidly, I hated myself when I did it — so insane and incomprehensible was such a death. My blows were senseless. (p. 106)

Once again the writer is aroused, insisting now that it makes no difference at all whether one dies without resistance as a broken man, or simply yields as a humble man. But the executioner persists in saying that it does. He has learned, he claims, something from such deaths. With great scorn the writer replies, "Ah! You learn even from the innocent whom you kill? That I call extremely utilitarian" (p. 106).

But the executioner persists in claiming that he has not forgotten a single one of those deaths and, in fact, thinks of nothing else. From such deaths he has learned the difference between what he can conquer and what is unconquerable; he has learned that in the end his power is limited.

> I can take your body, Sir; that force can ruin; for everything which decomposes into dust is subject to it. But that for which you fought, I have no power over it; for it does not belong to the dust. This is what I, an executioner, a despised person, have learned from the innocent, who are felled by my axe and who do not defend themselves. A person who, in the hour of his unjust death, lays aside his pride and anxiety — indeed, even his rights — in order to die as a child, without cursing the world, is a victor. . . . In the gentle yielding of the humble, in their peace, which encompasses even me as a prayer, in the monstrosity of their death, which contradicts all reason, in *this* thing which before the world is nothing but a laughing-stock, less even than a shrug of the shoulders, is revealed the powerlessness of injustice, death's lack of substance, and the reality of truth over which I can do nothing, which no executioner grasps and no prison encloses, of which I know nothing except that it *is*. (pp. 108-9)

The writer, infuriated, is not quite through. He screams, "Platitudes! Nothing but platitudes!" (p. 109). Yet he knows in his heart that this is the final question in the stark confrontation between the use of force to get one's way, and a goodness which will not use this force. It is either a question of platitudes, or the reality of an unbreakable truth. He is able to determine whether such goodness is invulnerable to force only by one act — the act of his allegiance to justice with humility.

In the face of this unabashed violence the writer chooses to die as he has lived — opposed to the unjust use of power. So as his final word he claims that it was a good thing that he resisted all along the exploitation of people. In so doing he did not seek to get his own way by force or coercion, but sought only to appeal to what was obviously just and good. For him to die humbly now is to continue to resist injustice. Now that the only power he has left is to choose *how* he will die, the writer will again use this power properly. He will yield to an unjust blow with humility. This is the paradox. By yielding to an unjust blow without pride or anxiety, he comes upon the goodness which is separated from injustice by a great chasm. Although the writer's throat will be cut, through an act of humble allegiance to justice he has found and joined himself to a goodness which cannot be touched by the force that will take his life.

It is at this point, the point at which violence and humility intersect, that he discovers the reality and nature of genuine goodness. Other people had been seekers after justice and, when they themselves were to be blotted out by an unjust use of power, died a truly imposing death by expressing their scorn and denunciation to the very last. This is not what is meant by humility. To join oneself by a *humble* allegiance to justice, to die without anxiety, pride, scorn, or denunciation when one is unjustly violated, leads to knowledge of, and participation in, a goodness which is beyond the reach of such a force. How a humble allegiance to justice leads to such goodness is not understood, but the fact that it is so can only be discovered by a suffering of injustice with humility. It is a commitment to suffer even to the extent of losing one's own life at the hands of that power which seeks to get its own way, rather than to resemble that power in any respect, by any form of self-aggrandizement. Such a response sees with utter clarity the unjust use of power for what it is, and by its humility is joined to a goodness that is otherwise separated from it by a great chasm.

II

My example from Dürrenmatt's play, that of a writer encountering his executioner, may help to show what genuine goodness is, and the fact that it is encountered through a humble refusal of the unjust use of power. Most of us are spared such naked confrontations, but all of us are in contact with this use of power to some degree. It can show itself in the most ordinary and mundane situations. When we have trouble getting what we want, we are tempted to use whatever means will serve to get it for us. The means we use to get our way can be as simple and as innocent as a charming smile, or a persuasive argument. But these are part of a continuum which may also include outright manipulation, or pressing a contract to the letter of the law, or telling a lie, until at the bottom of the scale we have the use of violence. A charming smile is not the same as a blow from an executioner's knife, but these are not separated by a gulf or a chasm. These two acts, and all that lies between them, are connected, however distantly, by the fact that each operates on the principle of getting what is desired — getting it unjustly, and without humility.

We do not usually seek to satisfy our desires unjustly at the outset. As infants and young children, many of our desires are met by our parents without our even having to ask. When we are older, and do have to act for ourselves in getting what we want, we still may not see that our methods — especially when the degree of injustice is mild — are connected by an unbroken series of steps to violence. Dürrenmatt's portrayal of the confrontation between executioner and writer may help us to see what getting our own way unjustly really amounts to, and that *all* injustice, however mild its appearance, is connected to a frightful kingdom. The stark example of the executioner and writer gives us the opportunity to see clearly the chasm which separates justice from injustice and, more important, to see that we have a decision to make regarding the way we shall seek to have our desires met. That is all we need see in order to decide where to place our allegiance — with that kingdom, or with another.

To seek to live justly leads to an increasing awareness, no matter how incomplete, of what genuine goodness is. This awareness is the first step toward participation in that goodness, and it can happen to some degree at any level of experience, not merely at the most extreme. The necessity of this decision, however, does involve us in a genuine dilemma. To renounce injustice in all its forms as a means of getting what we want does pose another question. Is this renunciation really the way to fullness of life? For some people, acting with justice may not involve severe hardship. Their circumstances of life may be such that they can get whatever they want by living and acting honorably. So there does not have to be an inevitable conflict between justice and the search for personal happiness.

But in Dürrenmatt's play, allegiance to justice and decency lead to the cutting of a writer's throat. It is hardly possible to say in his case that allegiance to justice led to fullness of life, at least not in a way that is apparent to us. This allegiance can in extreme cases lead to personal destruction and, in lesser cases, to various degrees of suffering. No one knows ahead of time what the outright rejection of injustice may entail.

So we can act with all justice in satisfying many of our desires and, if we are fortunate, never encounter a situation in which we must make the choice between continuing to act fairly or suffering severe losses. But it may happen. Indeed, it would probably happen more often than it does if we consistently lived as justly as we could, with our varying degrees of insight, understanding, justice, decency, and fairness. Nonetheless, a commitment to justice carries inherent risks, and these risks involve choices. We must be willing to renounce the satisfaction of at least some of our desires, even in the most favorable of circumstances, for the sake of justice. In very extreme cases, if we are firm in our commitment, we must find our only satisfaction in allegiance to what is just, and the genuine goodness to which it leads.

The route of desire and route of humility are connected to one another. Both involve an initial refusal, whether it be a refusal of desire, appetite, or a refusal of force in the fulfillment of this desire. The refusal we make in the first instance will help us to make it in the second. Otherwise we may well be led to despair when we lose something which matters greatly to us for the sake of justice, or when we are confronted by that stark, brute exercise of power to which no appeal is effective. When that happens, any claim for a goodness which is invulnerable to loss or violence may seem a matter of platitudes — just as it did to Dürrenmatt's protagonist. That is why we must make the first refusal, that by it we will have been prepared in advance to counter despair with belief in an indestructible goodness. Only thus can we remain firm, and do so with all humility. It is by means of such actions, and not by means of mere ideas, that we will come to recognize distinctive acts of goodness, the traces of God, at the time of our worst extremity.

PART TWO

OUR RESPONSE

What punishment is there, you ask, for those who do not accept things in this spirit? Their punishment is to be as they are.

Epictetus, *Discourses*

CHAPTER THREE

GRAVITY AND GRACE

The route of desire and the route of humility both involve a renunciation of finding fullness of life in our own way. The withdrawal of one's love from all that is earthly leads to the planting of God's seed of love, while the second renunciation — that of the use of force — helps us to an acceptance of our vulnerability to injustice. Those who suffer humbly know, by that very action, of an indestructible goodness, and come to participate in this goodness. The reality of such goodness, which is beyond the reach of injustice and brute power, we discover only by this act of humility.

Knowledge of the reality of this goodness is possible without a knowledge of God, just as the presence of the divine seed of love is possible quite apart from response and commitment to God. But they both serve as preparation for a recognition of God's goodness, that distinctive goodness invulnerable to injustice even in its most extreme form. Without such preparation the life of Jesus — the life of God incarnate — will seem to be a matter of platitudes. It will seem merely the story of a man who is good and who, when brutally executed, humbly yields himself up. So the reality of what is there will be overlooked; what Jesus *is* will not be properly seen.

Only if we have suffered and endured the same unjust use of power, in however small a degree, will we come to see the reality of an indestructible goodness in Jesus' suffering. By this act we will be able to recognize this goodness and to respond to it no matter where it occurs, and in whatever form it takes. By the same token a refusal of powerlessness, a refusal to perform such an action, will lead to a refusal of that recognition.

Only that part of the divine plane which intersects our own is perceptible; the rest is beyond our sight. If we have been prepared by our *actions* to recognize a distinctive goodness, then we may conceive the divine by means of *ideas* and so connect the invisible to the visible — human experience. The life of Jesus is just such an intersection: our ideas about divine love and goodness, and our participation in that goodness through the life and death of Christ.

The "ideas" I will use are largely taken from Simone Weil, a figure who is increasingly attracting attention both within and without religious circles. Simone Weil was born in Paris in 1909, and died during the Second World War at the age of thirty-four. Her parents were Jews, but not practicing Jews. From early childhood she combined intellectual brilliance with a profound concern for those who suffer. Weil was transferred from her first teaching post for leading a labor protest by unemployed municipal workers, and spent many hours as a volunteer teacher for railroad workers. She worked for a year in a car factory, and later spent several months working in the vineyards near Marseilles during the harvest in order to share the lot of those in lowly occupations. These jobs taxed her strength to the breaking point, as she was small, frail, and suffered from ill-health all her life. During the Civil War Weil went to Spain and enlisted in the anarchist brigade. All these experiences deeply influenced her writings, which amount to some ten volumes mostly published after her death.

I shall use her understanding of the Christian doctrines of creation and the cross, doctrines that involve ideas which describe the unseen part of the divine plane, and help delineate the nature of divine love and goodness present in Jesus. It is, however, the idea of Jesus as the *incarnation* of divine love and goodness which will enable me to describe the unique nature of the divine love of which Christianity speaks. It is that portrayal of the uniqueness of divine love and goodness which can lead us, once we have been properly prepared, to make our own response.

I

We cannot fully imagine the immense power needed to create a universe. But power is not enough; there is something beyond sheer power needed to create. To take an analogy from literature, Dorothy Sayers and Iris Murdoch both claim that the creation of characters for a story or novel requires some renunciation on the part of their creator. Writers must restrain their own personalities to create a personality which is not their own. In order that something may exist beyond and apart from themselves, they are required to renounce themselves. Good literature is no mere extension of a writer's personality, but entails an ethical act of self-renunciation so that something else might exist.

When God creates, it means that he allows something to exist which is not himself. This requires an act of profound renunciation. He chooses out of love to permit something else to exist, something created to be itself and to exist by virtue of its own interest and value. So the creation of a world means that God renounces his status as the only existent — he pulls himself back, so to speak, in order to give his creation room to exist for its own sake.

The physical universe God has created operates as it does without any choice. It forms an extremely complex order which we find not only useful, but intellectually satisfying. But our pleasure in the physical universe is more than an intellectual one. We also find it beautiful, and we take great delight in it even when we do not fully grasp the underlying order which causes this beauty.

In the opening chapter of *Gravity and Grace* Simone Weil states, "Two forces rule the universe: light and gravity."[3] She refers to the whole physical universe as the realm of this "gravity," and uses the term in a distinctive way. In science, gravity refers only to certain specific properties of matter. Weil, however, extends the term to refer to whatever acts automatically, according to its own nature. So she refers to the entire physical universe as the realm of gravity, since in it everything operates automatically, according to its nature, without any choice. Every piece of matter, every natural force, goes as far as it can until it is prevented by some external factor from going any further — unless it is an organism. An organism is subject to external limitation, as is an inanimate object like a rock, but it can also check its own action and limit its own growth. All expansion and self-limitation in the physical universe operates automatically, without the exercise of any choice.

In contrast to this realm of gravity there is another realm, one that Weil calls grace, or "light." Its basic characteristic is that it does not seek to go as far as it can; it does not expand until it is forced to stop by external or internal compulsion. Its hallmark is voluntary restraint. Restraint is exercised for the sake of other people and things, for it is a restraint that respects their reality. The very creation of the world is an act of such grace. God does not seek to be all that there is; he does not spread himself out, so to speak, to cover all that there is, but graciously pulls himself back to allow the world to exist. He voluntarily restrains himself, so there may be other realities. He holds himself back for the sake of the world. God *is* grace; the physical universe he has made is gravity.

There is no negative judgment implied in calling the physical world the realm of gravity. Things operate as they do innocently, because they have no freedom. To act according to their nature results in an orderly and beautiful universe, which delights both our intellect and our senses. In addition to this, the natural world is good. It is created, as I have said, out of love. God renounces his status as the only existent, that something else of value might exist in its own right, and he declares it good: "And God saw everything that he had made, and behold, it was very good" (Gen. 1:31).

Weil extends the term "gravity," furthermore, beyond the operations of the entire physical world and uses it as a way of describing human behavior. Even though human beings can act freely, she nevertheless sees an analogy between the operations of the physical universe and human conduct. "All the *natural* movements of the soul," she states, "are controlled by laws analogous to those of physical gravity. Grace is the only exception."[4] Usually, we exercise our freedom in a way that prevents us from communion with God. We tend to stay within the bounds provided by our natural endowments. We do not open ourselves to that communion with God which would empower us by grace to perform actions which transcend the bounds of these natural endowments. So as long as we do not have contact with God's grace, we are limited in all our actions to what our own given nature allows.

In addition to this limitation, the human personality has a further one similar to that of a machine. Just as a machine needs fuel to run, and will run out of fuel and stop unless this fuel is replaced, so too we need to have our energy for action constantly replenished from some source. It will be replenished either by the operation of our own nature or by the assistance of divine grace.

Simone Weil illustrates this with the example of a family, one of whose members is an invalid. The invalid is truly loved and cared for by the family, but in time resentment inevitably builds up because the supply of human love is limited. So the family does not have enough energy supplied by love to carry out the enormous task of taking care of an invalid year after year, day after day. The invalid is loved at the outset, but there simply is not enough fuel supplied from this source to keep on without drawing upon the energy that comes from resentment and self-pity. So the family members complain to each other, sympathize with each other, and this gives them some energy, or "fuel," to keep going.

Both the energy supplied by human love, and that supplied through resentment and self-pity, spring from our own nature. One is attractive; the other is not. The amount of each sort varies from person to person, but both arise out of human temperament and human makeup. Our need for fuel makes us automatically look for its replenishment. In taking care of a family member or helping a friend in need, people begin with the most excellent motives, combined with the admirable quality of human affection. But if they are called upon to make more effort than human love or affection can bear, then they are forced to draw upon the energy of less admirable motives. To illustrate this point, Simone Weil uses the analogy of people standing in line for food during a shortage: ". . . the people who stood, motionless, from one to eight o'clock in the morning for the sake of having an egg, would have found it very difficult to do so in order to save a human life."[5] To use another example, how often do we take on some charitable project out of sheer good intentions and then, as the

job becomes harder and harder, stick at it because of a far
different intention: we do not want the embarrassment of
other people knowing we gave up?

Consider another example Weil gives. She says that as
soon as one human being shows that he needs, really needs,
another, there is a tendency for the person so needed to
draw back. There are people to whom I can easily respond
when they express a need. Usually, however, the needs expressed are the kinds I *like* to meet, and from my response
I feel a kind of gratification, or fullness. The expenditure
of effort gets replenished, then, by the gratification I feel.
On the other hand, sometimes in the face of genuine need
my initial tendency is to remove myself, to get away. In
such a case I sense no possible return or gratification for
my effort; I just know instinctively that something is about
to be drained out of me, and I react automatically by trying to get away. It takes effort to overcome this automatic
response.

Weil claims that in all our actions there is a need to
receive the equivalent of what we give, even if it is only a
smile or a feeling of self-congratulation. We cannot bear
the emptiness that results from giving without any com-
pensation to help fill up the empty space. How resentful
and angry we feel when we get nothing for our efforts.
Have we not all felt and said with bitterness, "He did not
even say as much as 'thank you' for all that I did!" And we
do feel better for this expression of resentment. Energy is
restored by the sense of superiority which comes from fix-
ing our minds on the ingratitude or baseness of another
person.

Even though we obviously differ from the physical
universe in that our behavior arises out of the choices we
make, Weil uses the term "gravity" to refer to human behavior, in so far as our actions arise solely from our given

nature. So much of our thought and action is dominated by this need for "fuel." We act and think about others and ourselves in such a way as to protect ourselves from irreplaceable loss, to compensate ourselves for every expenditure of energy, and even to expand ourselves as far as we can until checked by something external or internal. We do this "naturally," that is to say, automatically.

As far as I am concerned, and here I may differ from Simone Weil, our gravity or nature is not *of itself* evil. Evil springs from the separation of our nature from the love of God, a separation that allows our desire for life, for expansion, and for self-exaltation to run its course, sometimes in evil and cruel directions. Our behavior is also limited to what our nature can do of and by itself, unless through our contact with God we are able to behave in ways beyond our natural power.

God has created us so that we can be connected to him, and he seeks that we, his creatures, love him and love one another. We can receive divine love, and through it allow our actions to be directed by his will and empowered by his grace. We can thus restrain our gravity from running its natural course, and rise above our limitations. Our natural powers thus become rightly directed and strengthened when connected to God's grace.

How this transformation of our gravity begins has already been described; it begins with the self's recognition of a void and an emptiness. If we renounce any hope of ever finding fullness, of ever gaining completeness by following the way of gravity alone — the pursuit of earthly things to feed our hunger — we imitate the very love of God which created the universe. He *voluntarily* enters upon an act of renunciation, that something besides himself might exist. We, too, are voluntarily to pull ourselves back. We are not forced to do so by anything external to us; certainly the world does not force us to recognize that it cannot fulfill us. The world yields to our pushes and pulls, yields to our discovery of its laws and our attempt to bend it to our own purposes. It yields to us, giving us all it can, for it has no choice. Nor is our self-restraint a matter of something internal to us; there is no dominant desire within us that forces us to renounce the world. What forces us is simply a recognition of the truth: we desire, but the world cannot fulfill us.

Then we are to wait, to suffer and endure that emptiness until God comes in secret and plants his seed. To wait is to allow grace its entrance, when a new principle is at work within us. Self-restraining grace is present and at work within the world, resident in our being. Love itself has entered a creation made from love. It finds its lodging in a creature, because that creature has restrained its desire for self-expansion and endured the emptiness which results. The action of its gravity, which apart from God's presence is at best limited and at worst destructive, is now capable of being redeemed, directed, and elevated by God's love.

II

With this idea of gravity and grace, we can now recognize the uniqueness of divine love and goodness. Creation is an act of love because it involves God's voluntary renunciation of himself as the only existent. The cross is Jesus' voluntary renunciation of himself. He is the victim of the forces of gravity — the expansion and aggrandizement of the Roman Empire, and the various aspirations of the Jewish Zealots, Temple authorities, Pharisees, and Sadducees. These forces of gravity, which together make a complex pattern of interlocking and conflicting systems, catch him up within their workings and crush him. Apparently forsaken by his Father, Jesus remains obedient to the realm of grace. He lays his life down humbly instead of following the way of force, of self-exaltation, and of blind assertion. That the gospel of John understands Jesus' humble acceptance of his death is indicated by the verse, "No one takes [my life] from me, but I lay it down of my own accord" (John 10:18). His death was caused by the actions of gravity, but in the grip of gravity's vise Jesus yields himself up voluntarily. He accepts his vulnerability to the forces of unrestrained gravity because he believes it to be his Father's will. Like the Suffering Servant in Deutero-Isaiah,

> He was despised and rejected by men;
> a man of sorrows, and acquainted with grief . . . .
> He was wounded for our transgressions,
> he was bruised for our iniquities;
> upon him was the chastisement that made us whole,
> and with his stripes we are healed. (Is. 53:3,5)

Thus is the love of the Creator — the love which restrained itself to permit the world's existence — answered from the cross by the Son. The Son renounces his own will by submitting to the power of creatures, and yields himself in faith that this renunciation is for our sake.

We have here a *unique* love portrayed. On the human plane we have someone unjustly and brutally executed, who endures death with humility; with the idea of incarnation placed in the context of creation and crucifixion, we have divine love, by which and through which all things were made. This love enters the creation and bears the destructive effects of creatures whose nature is no longer directed by the Creator's love. Divine love bears this as a creature, and bears it humbly. Such love is divine, a love that allows the creation its own freedom, and is willing to enter that realm as a creature to bear its ill effects.

The life of God thus reveals to us a unique love, and this revelation is sufficient for many to respond. The response comes about because love yields itself to love. Not everyone can make this response, however, because not everyone has been prepared for it in advance by the performance of certain actions. They have not renounced the world as a source of fullness, or they have not renounced power as a means of obtaining this fullness, and thereby discovered a goodness which they can recognize in Jesus' life and death. So the portrayal of Jesus as divine love does not enhance a goodness and a love they have previously known, nor drawn from them a response.

Even when we have been prepared to recognize the life of Jesus as the point where God intersects our own plane, we may still hold back from this recognition. There have always been a large number and variety of impediments that trouble us, from the problems of natural evil and human cruelty right down to the problem of the Bible's inspiration. To some of these problems, or stumbling-blocks, I want now to turn. I wish to stress, however, that these are only impediments, and impediments admit of release. They are barriers, or obstacles, that impede our recognition of God's life in our own, no less than the recognition of the life of God in Christ.

CHAPTER FOUR

SUFFERING AT THE HANDS OF NATURE

The laws which govern the natural world produce the immense beauty with which we are bathed on every side. There is apparently no magnification by a microscope which does not reveal this, nor any distance in space from which our earth does not look radiantly beautiful. Sensuous beauty, as I pointed out earlier, can be grasped by our intellect as well as by our senses. It can be reduced in part to the laws of physics and of chemistry, and thus become a source of great intellectual pleasure. It is the same world perceived by different means; the senses reveal sensuous beauty, the mind, intellectual beauty. Sensuous beauty is the radiance of nature's operation and order, the radiance of its laws and of its "gravity."

Although beauty fascinates both the eye and mind, it has no utility. We can only contemplate it, allow it to hold our attention and suggest to us some purpose, some finality, some completeness and perfection of immense importance. Yet that meaning, purpose, and perfection is always elusive; the beauty of the world constantly promises, yet it never satisfies. The very fact that beauty has no finality can suggest to us that the universe itself has no finality; that its purpose, if it has any, lies beyond it.

Earlier on we saw that we constantly crave, but can find nothing in the world which can finally satisfy us. The route of desire involves suffering, while beauty is another route to the same truth, namely, that what we seek is out-side the world. Beauty fills us with noble sentiments, seren-ity, expectancy. We wait and wait for something to feed upon, but beauty gently points us beyond itself and sug-gests to us that we should go beyond the world for finality. The contemplation of natural beauty, then, is another way we become receptive to the love of God, just as renuncia-tion of the world as a source of fullness can open us to God's presence.

The route of beauty is a joyous route, but if the seed of love is to remain in us and to grow, sooner or later we will have to face the suffering which comes from nature's operations. Nature's order, which a good deal of the time is sensuously and intellectually pleasant, can at the same time produce intense and brutal suffering. At such times we do not know how to connect our faith in God's good-ness with illnesses which cause the death of children, sense-less accidents, and natural catastrophes. They do not seem to go together, and when such catastrophes occur we do not know how we can reconcile God's love with intense human misery.

These evils are usually called "natural evils," caused as they are by the workings of nature. They are particularly troublesome since they cannot be explicitly linked to human freedom. It may be plausible to argue that a Chris-tian God and the existence of human evil are compatible because people have freely chosen to disobey God, and so suffer as a consequence. But the natural world has no such freedom; it operates as it does according to the laws given to it by God. When its operations harm us, neither sin nor evil can explain the distribution of such injuries. Everyone is a sinner, but only some people suffer, and injuries are not distributed according to people's relative merits. "For [your Father] makes his sun rise on the evil and on the good, and sends rain on the just and on the unjust" (Matt.

5:45). Microbes attack the just as readily as the unjust; the good are killed or injured in senseless accidents, just as the morally culpable are.

Often in the face of the inexplicability of suffering we simply "hang on," trusting in God's goodness even though there are ills which do not seem to make sense. I do not want to belittle or dismiss the response of hanging on, for often this is all that we can do; sometimes, however, we can actually do more. Suffering at the hands of nature may be an opportunity for *contact* with God. Sometimes in the midst of suffering we receive a gracious presence. Even on the occasions when we do not, we can still act redemptively if we have the conviction that Christ's response to his own suffering was redemptive. Experiencing God's gracious presence in the midst of our suffering and taking part in a positive redemptive act do not normally come about without some preparation. The nature and effects of suffering must be reflected upon, and acted upon rightly, so that the experience of suffering itself may be redemptive.

I

Most of our thoughts and actions are self-serving. We stand at the center, with all other people and events in orbit around ourselves. Everything is seen from our perspective and is evaluated, understood, and thought about in such a way as to enhance, comfort, or protect ourselves. We do this as automatically as matter and energy perform their operations. But sometimes we rise above our egotism; however rarely, and however imperfectly, we do at times restrain our self-concern.

One way this can occur is through the fact that we are material beings. We are part of the natural physical order, subject to its laws, subject to microbes and viruses, subject to aging and decay, and subject to death. We encounter here certain realities that we cannot always avoid — we can mitigate them, but we cannot entirely avoid them. How do we react to the fact that we are material beings, subject to wear and tear? How do we react to illness, to accident, to decay, to death? Do we respond egotistically? Most of the time we do, asking, "Why did this happen to me? What did I ever do wrong?" This is often said, and often enough felt, with a sense of indignation or outrage or self-pity. I certainly feel this way when — try as I may — things do not go well for my own children, while I see other people's children who have been neglected getting along splendidly. At other times, when we feel that we suffer adversity unfairly, we can become mute with depression. These are just some examples drawn from a host of quite automatic and normal reactions to adversity.

But these automatic responses can be the occasion for reflection, an occasion to ask oneself: "Why did I think that good and evil are parcelled out according to some scheme of merit, when the book of Job so clearly teaches the opposite, and Jesus Christ himself suffered so shamefully?" Such reflection may lead us to recognize more fully something we already know: as material beings, as pieces of matter, we are vulnerable to injury, illness, and decay. To realize this is to realize our status and our place in the universe, and to realize what we are. It is to come to terms with a hard fact.

At the same time this realization also helps to transcend the psyche's self-serving mechanism. Such egocentricity seeks to expand, to get its own way, to go as far as it can. When the flow of our self-regard is painfully interrupted, however, reflection can lead to a new awareness of our limitations, and it may even lead to our acceptance of such limitations. The achievement of any degree of humility is to have performed an act that no other material being has the capacity to perform. Paradoxically, our automatic response to suffering, which on reflection yields to a more realistic recognition of what we are, also enables us to recognize that we have by that very act transcended being *merely* a piece of matter. We are not encompassed completely by the principles that govern the rest of matter; in this sense, we are spiritual beings. For this reason, our spirituality is found and affirmed precisely in and through the very fact that we are material beings, subject to the grinding wear and tear of matter. In facing the hard facts of illness, accidents, decay, and death we can rise above our egotism to discover that we are spiritual beings.

In a poem entitled "Common Life," Ray Lindquist portrays just such a response to the hard facts of our material vulnerability.

> Waiting for a lab report,
> Dependent on mysterious authorities,
> Gazing at my daughter in hospital,
> Her mother and I sharing a hard fellowship,
> I know a timeless, tribeless circumstance:
> I drive to the hospital in an eternal procession,
> I eat in the snack bar among the whole human race;
> My tears began 100,000 years ago
> And will never stop.6

The speaker in this poem moves from his own grief and his own concern to his inclusion in the grief of the whole human race. He is able to see his daughter's illness, as well as his own pain, as part and parcel of the vulnerability of the whole human race. His tears are part of all the tears ever shed. His drive to the hospital is not merely his own journey, but part of an "eternal procession"; the meal he eats is in the company of the whole human race. It is no accident that Lindquist has called his poem "Common Life," as it has to do with human solidarity and common human suffering. Through the experience of his daughter's suffering the speaker transcends the laws of his own gravity.

So the fact of our material vulnerability can be the occasion that moves us off-center, and melts the illusion of our immense significance, to show us we are but dust and ashes. This is part of the truth about us. Yet in that very recognition, in the very act of being humbled, we see that we are spiritual beings. To say in the face of hard realities simply, "Yes, it is so," is to exhibit a capacity not found in the rest of matter. The Greek Stoic philosopher, Epictetus, stresses this kind of humility. He regards human beings, particularly himself, as part of the cosmos with no special privileges except these — to perceive that the cosmos is orderly, to give thanks for its positive benefits, and to endure its destructive force without degradation. He did not know that this was a preparation for something greater.

II

The preparation I have described makes it possible, even in the face of acute suffering, for us to perform a further action, a further yielding to the facts of our vulnerability as creatures. We can yield ourselves to God and, in that act of yielding, find our spirits met by God. Sister Basilea Schlink, the founder of a Protestant order of nuns, *Marienschwestern,* near Darmstadt, West Germany, tells us "when you are in suffering say, 'Yes, Father,' and strength will flow into your heart."[7] She offers this statement not as a theory, but as a description of what actually happens when we so yield. Edith Barfoot, who spent seventy of her eighty-seven years in suffering, also speaks of her experience of a gracious presence. Rheumatoid arthritis deprived her of her power of movement, her eyesight, and, ultimately, her hearing. She says that as a young girl she wanted to be a nurse, but found that her vocation was to be a patient. Significantly, her book is entitled *The Joyful Vocation to Suffering,* a book in which she celebrates the call of God to this vocation, and the gracious presence of God she found in the midst of her suffering.[8]

Such a graciousness cannot be known theoretically. It comes only through the action of affirming God's rule; nature operates either of its own accord, or under the authority of another. In saying "Yes, Father" to the unavoidable necessities of life, we submit to nature's might as something under God's oversight and rule, and not merely as a senseless, destructive force. Through this act of faith, the gracious presence of God is known; it flows into us and bestows a felicity that is beyond the calculation of the pluses and minuses of the pleasant and unpleasant things of this life. The goodness of God cannot be spoken of solely in terms of health, strength, and well-being, and simply set over against the untoward things which have happened or may happen. God himself is good, a unique good, whose value cannot be compared to the creaturely benefits and evils we know.

The act by which we say, "Yes, Father," and yield to nature's might as something ruled by God, is not necessarily an act of which we are aware. It is the action Simone Weil performed when she suffered from intense headaches and recited, as she sometimes did during those times, George Herbert's poem, "Love." Without realizing it, she claims, she was actually praying.

> Christ himself came down and took possession of me. . . . I had never foreseen the possibility of that, of real contact, person to person, here below, between a human being and God. . . . Moreover, in this sudden possession of me by Christ, neither my senses nor my imagination had any part; I only felt in the midst of my suffering the presence of a love.[9]

There had been for her a long preparation for this reception of Christ's presence, even if the preparation was not an action consciously undertaken. Part of this preparation was her having to learn, bit by bit, the lesson of her material vulnerability. In no case is the act whereby we yield to nature's might, as something over which God is sovereign, simply a matter of reading a chapter such as this and saying on the next occasion of an illness, "Yes, Father." We must first learn to see that nature is an orderly whole, with each part operating as it does — without any regard for any other part. We must face our vulnerability to its workings, and allow the fact of our vulnerability to form part of the substance of our character. Then we may be ready to yield ourselves to nature as a reality under the authority of the Father — and to yield completely. That "yes, Father" is what people such as Schlink, Barfoot, and Weil claim leads to a reception of a gracious love in the midst of our sufferings.

III

Now I come to a most difficult matter, one which amounts to a further impediment. What can we do when we suffer at the hands of nature but feel no gracious presence, even if we have already accepted the fact of our vulnerability and, paradoxically, our capacity to transcend it? We may well have experienced God's presence in the midst of suffering on other occasions, but what if in a particular instance we feel no gracious presence? Does it mean we have been abandoned, turned over to nature's destructive force, and God no longer has contact with us?

No. God is still sovereign over nature, and therefore we can maintain indirect contact with him through its workings. Of course we do not feel God's love through nature; we feel only pain, as if he were utterly absent. It is as if we had been abandoned and left to nature's mercy.

When this happens the situation can go in two different directions, depending on what our actions are. We can use this as an opportunity to reject the idea of God's love and God's rule, because they are not evident to us in this particular case of suffering. This rejection can take many different forms and be of various degrees of intensity, ranging all the way from mere abstract disbelief to utter despair. To move in the other direction is to trust God, to have faith in the fact that he rules, that we are not beyond his reach despite what nature inflicts. We can trust that nothing nature inflicts can separate us from the love of God, even when we feel forsaken. This can be done probably only by a person who has performed at least the first act we have described, and probably more easily by a person who has performed both.

The nature and quality of the suffering itself is affected by whichever direction we take, for our act of response becomes part of the *total event.* An act of rejection affects the total event in one way; an act of trust affects it in another. So what we do matters. By our own act we can, at the very least, prevent what is negative — suffering without any sense of God's presence — from becoming more negative. If we are led to reject God, then the total event has no redemptive features at all. If we can hold on to our trust, at least the total event is not one in which faith in God's love has been relinquished.

The basis for trust in such situations is our knowledge of the suffering Jesus endured on the cross. Even though his affliction was caused by human action, it still happened only because he was a vulnerable piece of matter which could be nailed to wood, could bleed and die. But to show a connection between Jesus' suffering and our own, especially the suffering we undergo at nature's hands, it is necessary to present several ideas.

First, the Son and the Father are one God through their love for one another before the foundation of the world. The Son, when he became incarnate, also became separated by a great distance from the Father. "Distance" is a metaphor; it specifies what is subject to the forces of nature in contrast to what is not. The incarnate Son, while he is in the world, is subject to natural forces; the Father is not. They are separated by the "distance" of the created world. In saying that the Son is subject to natural forces, I mean that he is subject to the pull of physical gravity, and the need to eat and to breathe. Jesus can only command nature through the Father; he cannot do so by his powers alone.

Second, many of the events produced by the laws of nature and by human actions are pleasant to us; some are not. Some can make us suffer greatly, and the most serious suffering of all we call "affliction." One of the most profound analyses of the nature of affliction ever given is that of Simone Weil, based largely on her experience with factory work and with refugees during the Second World War.[10] According to Weil, affliction is a very specific form of suffering. It can be caused by physical suffering, if this suffering is very prolonged or frequent. But the affliction of which she speaks is not primarily that bound up with physical suffering. To be "afflicted" is to be uprooted from the fabric of social relations and no longer to count for anything; it is nakedness, loss of status, and social degradation. What makes the quality of affliction worse is the inner feeling of contempt and disgust for oneself, which corresponds to the expressed contempt of others towards those who, socially, do not figure. People thus afflicted feel this contempt and disgust, as well as guilt and even defilement, in proportion to their innocence.

Christ is described in the New Testament as one who is "afflicted." He endures brutal physical treatment from the soldiers who beat him, march him to Golgotha, and nail him to the wood of a cross. He endures not only great pain, but also humiliation, stripped of all social status by his conviction as a common criminal. Jesus' shame includes the soldiers' mockery when they clothe him in a robe of royal purple and pretend to bow down to him as a king. As he hangs from the cross, the priests, scribes, and elders shout, "He saved others; he cannot save himself" (Matt. 27:42). This comment must have raised a roar of laughter. Jesus' words, the words of Psalm 22, "My God, my God, why hast thou forsaken me?" suggest the degree to which he experienced utter abandonment. He can be said to have been driven the greatest possible distance from the Father; in St. Paul's words, "For our sake he made him to be sin who knew no sin, so that in him we might become the righteousness of God" (II Cor. 5:21). Holiness and sin are separated by an infinite distance from one another.

Third and most important, the distance between the Father and the Son can also be thought of as the exact measure of their love. The Son is afflicted by the Father for our sakes; he enters the world, is made subject to it, and is crucified to establish contact between what is subject to nature and to sin, and what is not. All this is brought about through the Father's loving will.

The Son's great victory is to yield to the will of his Father; thus they are united over the great span of distance, because there is love at each extremity. Their distance from one another thus becomes a measure of the extent of their love, expressed by the very medium of their separation. Christ's pain is real pain; his affliction is horrible. Yet he responds to it as the will of the Father, and this affliction is unable to break the contact between himself and his Father.

Earlier we saw that contact between what is and what is not a creature is possible through the medium of the created world. We saw that by yielding to nature's power as subject to the rule of God, we receive a gracious presence. In a situation where no gracious presence is felt, we can still believe in God's love by seeing that "distance," understood as the ordered cosmos between us and God, can also be a form of nearness. If we respond to nature as *his* creation, then we are connected. God's love exists on the far side of nature, and faith in his love exists on this side. The universe between God and us thus becomes a medium of contact. The pressure of the world provides an indirect contact with God, its ruler. When nature's touch is pleasant, this indirect contact is also pleasant; when nature hurts us, we still have an indirect contact with the Father. However horrible it may be, we can have faith that we are still in contact with a loving Father, no matter how many other forces have intervened. His Son went the greatest possible distance, and was not by that distance separated from his Father's love.

Reflection on Christ's affliction thus gives us a basis for action, for bringing some redemptive element into a negative situation. By humble faith we can actually affect and change the total situation in which we are caught up. We can continue to love even when the love of God is veiled by the unpleasant pressure of nature, and the result is a more perfect love of God. There is always a role we can play in our own suffering; not utterly powerless, we can bring a new element to the total situation and make it different from what it would otherwise be. God still provides us with a way to act redemptively. We have not been driven utterly beyond this possibility, but by our own action can mitigate the evil of unavoidable suffering.

Again, this is not a theoretical matter, though it can be formulated intellectually, and such formulation may assist us. Above all, there is an action to be performed, and the act can take many different forms. A man dying of cancer, for example, may have only one great unresolved anxiety: what will happen to his young family? The realization that he is failing to trust his Father, whose love he has known in other forms and under other circumstances, may cause this anxiety to slide from his shoulders like a great weight. He can yield his family to his Father's care and be free of paralyzing worry; in this way, the total situation is altered from what it otherwise would have been. Similarly, those who suffer nature's grip vicariously, through their concern for others, can by their actions affect the total situation. They can shape the entire event of which they are a part, and make it better or worse by their own response of faith in God's love.

I have not sought to explain why there are natural evils, but simply tried to show how we can do more than simply "hang on" in the face of them. All three actions I have described are probably beyond where most of us are in our spiritual development. Most of us have probably made some progress only with the first: we have found ourselves more humble, even if only temporarily, in the face of nature's rough handling. Even so, it is of great value to have the witness of those who have gone further. Such testimonies enable us to understand how the love of God so gloriously displayed in the beauty and order of nature and in the life and teaching of his Son can also be known in the adversities we suffer, and so keep us from losing heart so easily.

The portrayal of the Son as separated by a distance from his Father, and for this distance to be a measure of their love, also further deepens our understanding of the nature of divine love. We see that the Son is able to enter the world and be afflicted for our sakes, and yet for all this nothing can destroy the love of the Son for the Father. The perception of such love may overcome impediments to a confession of divine love as creator and incarnate redeemer for those of us who have been prepared by the love and goodness we have known in other ways.

CHAPTER FIVE

SUFFERING HUMAN CRUELTY

We have seen that divine love can reach us in the midst of suffering caused by the operations of the natural world. But what of the suffering visited on us by human beings? It is often said that such suffering is caused by people's misuse of their freedom. God is not responsible for the suffering; he merely permits it by allowing people to be free. I believe this to be essentially true, but it does not deal with the question of the distribution of suffering. Admirable people sometimes suffer greatly at the hands of others. Innocent people have been victimized, persecuted, tortured, and killed, and why this is so we do not fully understand. Christian believers are often troubled by it, and it can seriously impede those otherwise attracted to Christianity from becoming Christians.

This chapter is not an attempt to solve this mystery of the distribution of suffering, nor to explain human cruelty. But I will try to show that people have experienced the love of God even in the most extreme circumstances of human cruelty, and been driven so close to Christ that he and he alone has become the rock on which they stand.

This is to have gone a step farther than the writer in Dürrenmatt's radio play, who found a goodness beyond the reach of the executioner's knife. In this case the extremity is so great that a new *identity* is found, an identity based on identification with Christ himself. This identification with Christ does not justify the existence of human cruelty, nor is it an attempt on my part to explain why God allows it. But it does show that the love of God can be found even in a place where one would least expect to find it.

I want to consider a concrete instance of this kind of experience by looking at two books by Iulia de Beausobre — *The Woman Who Could Not Die,* which is autobiographical, and *Creative Suffering,* a more general account of the presence of divine love in the midst of suffering.[11] I will try to show that what she experiences and describes is applicable to every believer in ordinary life, even those who have never been forced to encounter and endure such severe human cruelty.

I

Iulia de Beausobre was arrested and tortured in Russia during the early 1930's, when millions suffered and perished under Stalin's ruthless purges and forced collectivization of farms. For three months she lived in solitary confinement, followed by three more months in the "Inner" — as the worst part of the prison was called. People around her thought it miraculous that she endured this experience and came out mentally and morally intact, as the duration of such treatment was usually no more than six weeks. Once her interrogation was over, de Beausobre was used as a guinea pig for medical experiments. Finally she was sentenced to five years in a hard labor camp, but was released after a year because she was too ill to be capable of any kind of work.

On the surface, it would appear to be a situation from which nothing of value could emerge. Worst of all were the confrontations prisoners had to face from teams of examining officers, who zealously and sadistically sought to reduce everyone to mere instruments that performed on command, creatures devoid of personal will. In *Creative Suffering* de Beausobre is careful to make the point that there is no masochism in her claim that such suffering can be creative. There is no pleasure in suffering the isolation of solitary confinement, separated from the normal rhythms of life, from the sight of the sky, until the silence itself becomes agonizingly "audible." Her eyes, subjected to the merciless glare of an intense naked light bulb, become so painful that a cloth soaked in tea, though only giving momentary relief, nonetheless produces near ecstasy. Steady physical deterioration saps her morale, and forces her to begin to question her personal identity.

> Am I really this wretched pasty-faced, hollow-cheeked, insufficiently clean person with sunken eyes, lying on a narrow spiky camp-bed in a room completely bare but for a bed, a large two-tiered table, and a huge metal bucket with a lid to it in the corner nearest the door?[12]

Such physical suffering is arranged by Examining Officers, who take a deep and intimate delight in the suffering of those they question. Working in teams, with carefully planned interrogations lasting for hours, these officers produce a rhythm of fear and hope that breaks down the prisoners' defenses and drives them to the edge of madness. Under such circumstances, what can a person do?

> When you are in direct contact with this type of mind, you very soon learn that there is only one way to make your torturers stop torturing you, and that is to become invulnerable.

How can a person become invulnerable?

> To a sadist you are of interest only for a particular series of reactions which he makes it his business and pleasure to provoke from you. . . . For the victim there is only one way open

to save himself, and that is to fail to react at all: then, having ceased to be interesting, he will eventually be left alone.[13]

It is at this point, however, that the greatest danger arises. An individual may cease to react by becoming completely passive, completely unfeeling, like the victims of Dürrenmatt's executioner, "who yield their lives like dumb animals."

> This easier way involves rendering yourself completely unfeeling. It can be done: and once it is achieved, your tormentors weary in time, and your immediate aim is thus gained.

The price of this gain is great. Those who pay this price "become clod-like, indifferent, sub-human. . . . If you once lapse into such a condition, it is unlikely that you will ever get out of it. . . ."[14]

The other way for the victim to become invulnerable to sadism involves intense action. It requires a close attention to one's surroundings, even the details, and the victim must not seek to escape suffering by becoming unreceptive to what is outside.

> I may not dull myself to my surroundings any longer. If I do the penalty of idiocy lies ahead.

Yet to be attentive means, by necessity, an intense awareness of the horror being inflicted.

> Can I experience the acuteness of all this sordidness without hating life and man? Can I possibly bear it with equanimity?
>
> The effort of keeping a clear awareness of my surroundings makes me go cold with clammy sweat. I set my teeth hard so they will not chatter.[15]

The victim must also seek to penetrate, as far as possible, into the minds of the cross-examiners. This is especially hard because clear insight into another person's mind always requires a cultivation of sympathy, and sympathy can easily become sentimentality. So there can be no slurring-over of the responsibility borne by the tormentors. Finally, all passions such as self-pity, fear, and despair must be controlled, because they severely upset clarity of perception as one tries to penetrate the minds of those causing the torment, and tries to understand the tormentors as people.

There is no claim, and no expectation, that everyone can do this. But for those who do, such an effort has two results.

> You realize that you have been privileged to take part in nothing less than an act of redemption. And then you find that, incidentally and inevitably, you have reached a form of serenity which is, if anything, more potent to counteract sadistic lusts than any barren impassivity could be. But to your mind, now, that is a minor matter. The direct and positive work of an effort applied in this way towards redeeming the deed is far too big and too thrilling for anything else to matter to you very much at the moment.16

How is this an act of redemption? De Beausobre explains it in a passage where she imagines a conversation between herself and what she calls her "Leonardo." "Leonardo" is the person she aspires to become.

> A great bond is formed, he says, between the man who is tortured day in, day out, and the man who day in, day out, tortures him. Greater than there could possibly be between the tortured man and a blithe free citizen who understands nothing because he does not want to see or know a thing. If you ponder on this you may find the justification for your apparently absurd suffering.
>
> But, Leonardo, surely there is no justification for a crowd of well-fed, reasonably strong men bullying a weary, undernourished, half-demented woman who doesn't even know what it is all about.

. . . If you want to understand, to know the truth about this sort of thing, you must rise higher and look deeper. If you do, you can transform the ghastly bond into that magic wand which changes horror into beauty. . . . It is unpardonable that anyone should be tortured, even you — if *you* merely leave it at that. But, surely, when you overcome the pain inflicted on you by them, you make *their* criminal record less villainous? Even more, you bring something new into it — a thing of precious beauty. But when, through weakness, cowardice, lack of balance, lack of serenity, you augment your pain, their crime becomes so much the darker, and it is darkened by you. If you could understand this, your making yourself invulnerable would not be *only* an act of self-preservation; it would be a kindness to *Them*. . . . Look right down into the depths of your heart and tell me — Is it not right for you to be kind to them? Even to them? Particularly to them, perhaps? Is it not right that those men who have no kindness within them should get a surplus of it flowing towards them from without?

The whole of me responds with a "Yes!" like a throb of thundering music. It is so shattering that it makes me stagger. The jailer steadies me: "Take care!". . . . Drowsily I think: 'Oh, Leonardo, what if we are both only mad after all, my dear?'[17]

This passage has many points which can help us understand the extraordinary outcome de Beausobre claims can result from an active response to human cruelty. To start with, there is the bond between the tortured and the torturer; they do not remain isolated from one another, but become a part of each others' lives. Together they are part of *one event,* and the meaning and significance of this event is partly in the hands of the tortured person. For this reason, the victim is not utterly helpless. It is up to her to affect what that event shall be, and in this way affect what every participant in that event is, as well as what each has done. Because the tormentors are bonded to the victim, what they become depends in part on what the victim does. If she breaks, or becomes as indifferent as a lump, their crime is even greater. But the victim has the power to make this crime less vile than it might be, by allowing a new and precious element to enter into the event itself — a kindness, a peace, a love that overflows.

But immediately after de Beausobre has responded to this opportunity with a thundering "Yes!", she feels herself to be on the edge of madness, and then of despair. Nothing seems to matter — including this opportunity.

> Out of the icy wilderness of utter indifference, out of the shattering, all-embracing, chill understanding that wrecks all feeling of security, one flame calls in a limitless dark universe. One flame that still hovers within my iced body, burning bright and straight as the flame of a taper before the Crucifix. Then all in me dies.18

It is then that Christ reveals himself, and she finds in him her security, her invulnerability, and a warmth which not only elevates her with joy, but enables her to love. Through the very intensity of her suffering, through the being stripped of all that has hitherto constituted her personality — her past, her future hopes, her appearance, her temperament, her likes and dislikes — de Beausobre enters into the presence of Christ. Now she is only a nameless "something" which, uprooted from all else, is bonded to Christ. She has become invulnerable.

> The past-masters of psychology who hold you in their power, do all they can to shatter you completely. One of their avowed objects is to 'recondition' their victims . . . [their methods] gradually uproot all previous conditioning and lay bare the deepest layers of your subconscious. This no one can escape or fight against. And it is therefore vital for you to feel and know beyond all possible doubt that, notwithstanding all the tormentor's devices, there is, and always will remain, within you something that is built on rock. That this something cannot be torn out of you or severed from the rock, because it is the core of your personality and one with the rock it is built on. Being both of you and of the rock and not being anywhere outside of you or the rock, it cannot be uprooted. Besides, being of eternity, the more it is laid bare, the brighter it shines.19

The rock is Christ, and this "something" she describes is the experience of an emptiness at the core of oneself, the experience I described in the first chapter. This emptiness must always be attached to something else, attached either to all that makes up our personality, or attached to the love which made all things. De Beausobre has been uprooted and exposed, stripped of her friends, her work, her place in society — of everything that formerly made her herself. Such affliction could have broken her; she could not be a person when stripped to a bare "something." But to one who reaches that point is given the awareness that the only true identity is in Christ, through joining the divine love which itself travelled the extreme distance of affliction.

The self, the core, is left with no identity of its own beyond the rock to which it is bound and upon which it rests. It then becomes true for de Beausobre, as it was true for St. Paul, that "it is no longer I who live, but Christ who lives in me . . ." (Gal. 2:20). The divine love is her own life, and her own will. Of such a person it can be said, "For you have died, and your life is hid with Christ in God" (Col. 3:3). In this horrible travail, something of precious beauty has come into the world — the divine presence. This entire event of the brutal torture of an innocent person has become the union between that creature and divine love. This union is a part of the entire event, as the crucifixion of Jesus is more than an unjust, brutal death because of Jesus' response.

In addition, this precious new thing — divine love now present in this woman — goes forth from her to others. The guards respond to her by treating her with respect, and they even try to please her in small ways. When her period of solitary confinement is over, the prison physician mentions her cell block with admiration; there, the prisoners do exercises to keep their strength up, and clean their cells with pride. Their "gravity" — their own individual qualities — return, but this gravity is directed by the love at the center of their lives, and thus elevated by it.

Even de Beausobre's interrogators are affected. In her capacity as a victim, she has found another source of power. By paying full attention to what is taking place, by seeking to understand her tormentors without letting understanding degenerate into sentimentality, she has made them face the reality of what is going on — a morally outrageous act. If she had broken down and hence cooperated with them, or returned hatred for evil, this would have obscured the reality of the situation and, for her tormentors, the enormity of their deeds.

That is precisely what happens in the Dürrenmatt play. The executioner responds to the scorn of those who protest against injustice and tyranny with blows: "It was me against them." So the reality of what was taking place was lost on him through the byplay of "gravity" encountering "gravity." Only by encountering the humble does the executioner recognize the horror of his acts, and the reality of a goodness beyond the reach of the power which he wields.

So too in the case of de Beausobre. Her response does not result in a *personal* struggle between herself and her tormentors, which would merely hide from them all recognition of their cruelty. Far from distracting them from this reality, de Beausobre's response forces them to recognize that she is indeed a victim, and that they are perpetrating evil. Her oppressors encounter genuine goodness, for their knowledge of this evil is, paradoxically, the first step in their redemption. The reality of good and evil has been made available to them by her suffering. De Beausobre does not "excuse" them either by succumbing to their power or by reacting with automatic hatred and scorn.

Her chief tormentor, when he informs her that they are finished with her, and that she will now be executed, also says,

> "I should like you to be quite clear on one point. We only kill those of whom we think very highly and those whom we despise profoundly. You cannot doubt that we think highly of you."

This terrible irony, this strange mixture of evil and respect, is not a lovely thing. It differs significantly, however, from a situation of unmitigated horror — even to us, who only view it from a distance. De Beausobre, a participant, replies to his statement with, "I shall console myself with that when I am dying."

> We smile. We both like the answer, the sound of it coming after his words. When you have sunk to the lowest depths the surface of things acquires new values.[20]

As a participant she can tell us from experience how she can respond as she does.

> The tone of fortitude shown by the tortured is very different when they think of themselves only as poor, or brave, lonely wretches and when they think of themselves as members of the mystical body of Christ. Only the latter are likely to come through without succumbing to hatred. Moreover, it is only they who can pool their terrible experiences with the redemptive work of others. They alone can raise their harrowing experience from the level of a personal evil, or even of a personal matter at all, and make of it an impersonal enrichment, a universal good, a part of the redemptive work of Christ in his mystical body — the Church. [Under such extreme trial] it is difficult, if you love God at all, not to love him to the exclusion of man, difficult not to fly to him as a refuge from detestable mankind.[21]

To be able to love one's neighbor in these circumstances one must receive divine love not only directly from

God, but also indirectly from those who bear it within themselves. In the moment of her deepest trial, de Beausobre heard these words, "Seek in the miracle of warmth flowing from harrowed man to harrowed man. Seek and you will find me."[22] To her surprise, the first person from whom she experiences the flow of divine love is the governor of the prison. This is a man who lives with the daily agony of supervising a place of evil, trying as best he can, and at great personal risk, to mitigate in small ways the wretchedness of the prisoners. He arranges for more ventilation to reduce the stench of the cells, struggles to find books for the prisoners and, whenever he dares, looks at them with eyes of compassion. De Beausobre encounters this love also in the other prisoners who share her cell, and in numerous encounters that take place when she is transferred to a hard labor camp. Throughout both books, she insists that her experience of divine love in the midst of suffering is not unique.

In *Creative Suffering,* the author describes the spiritual outlook of the Russian people in order to explain how her experience of redemptive action and the presence of divine love is not an experience unique to herself. That outlook

> takes it for granted that any and every deed of ugliness can and should be redeemed and transfigured, and that, in all ordinary circumstances, a man must participate in the deed done, if he is to participate in its redemption.[23]

A person must encounter evil, feel its effects, and by his or her response form a bond between the sufferer and the one who causes the suffering. Then even the one who causes suffering can participate to some degree in divine grace, the grace that comes into the world through the followers of Christ. The servants of Christ are to bear a cross as their master did; he was not remote, but came down

from heaven and suffered greatly, to transfigure and redeem us who are bound to sin. Evil cannot exist without
causing suffering, and often it does go unredeemed. It cannot be redeemed unless those who are evil are met by those
who bear within them divine love, and by this love become
bonded to them.

It is no accident that de Beausobre and her fellow
Christians in prison used to hear and tell each other stories
of the lives of great saints. To speak of the saints was to
speak of that great multitude to which they belonged
through sharing in the same divine love. They belonged to
that great work of redemption, part of the kingdom which
breaks into the earthly plane and which, by God's power
and will, is to permeate and redeem all that is earthly.

II

We have seen by this examination of de Beausobre's
writings how the love of God can reach us even in the most
horrible circumstances of human cruelty. Christ's peace
and strength can enable us to become invulnerable even to
the most sadistic tortures. In fellowship with one another,
the prisoners among whom de Beausobre lived found
themselves able to resist feelings of hatred toward their
enemies. This is not unlike the response I described in the
previous chapter, the response by which we, in the midst of
the seeming animosity of the natural world, can experience
the presence of a divine love.

De Beausobre also shows how our response to human
cruelty gives us the opportunity to participate in Christ's
redemptive work. This, too, is similar to the sufferer's
response to nature I described, a response which can affect
the nature of the total situation and make it better or worse.

De Beausobre, however, emphasizes the joy and thrill of having taken part in a redemptive act. There is no parallel to this joy in our response to nature's adverse effects; the reason for this lies in the difference between the natural world and human beings. The natural world is innocent, with no freedom of action, whereas people are responsible for what they do. To take part in their redemption to the slightest degree, or even to mitigate the horror of what they do by one's own response, is to do something of eternal significance.

De Beausobre's works also reveal several other matters of value to us who have not personally suffered from extreme human cruelty. First, the description of being stripped of all that makes one distinctive helps us to see what Jesus endured on the cross. After de Beausobre has been stripped of her past and future, possessions and friends, she becomes a person who in her deepest moments of torment has no distinctive traits. She becomes indistinguishable from other brutally treated people, all of them battered pieces of anonymous flesh.

All of us have distinctive characteristics which lend us an identity, but human cruelty drives its victims toward the same experience of anonymity that Christ suffered. He was unjustly tried, convicted, and executed among criminals. His prime identity became one shared only by criminals. This may open our eyes to see more clearly the nature of Jesus' crucifixion, and thus to see more clearly the distinctive nature of divine love. Divine love is willing to go all lengths — reduced at first to the status of a criminal, and finally to a broken lump of flesh. Paradoxically, this anonymity becomes a *distinctive* characteristic of divine love.

Reflection on human cruelty also shows us something about ourselves, which is not as visible by other means. The route of desire can reveal to us a hunger that nothing of this world can feed, an emptiness, a "nothing," at our core. The route of humility can show us a genuine goodness beyond the reach of physical violence, a goodness in which we may participate. The route of beauty can suggest to us that any finality we seek lies beyond this world. Suffering at the hands of nature helps us see that we are spiritual beings, who can know God's love in the midst of suffering and through this love can act redemptively. But reflection on human cruelty gives us a deeper understanding of our own identity — of what and who we actually are.

Through this reflection we come to learn that we are creatures with a need to be bonded to something beyond ourselves in order to possess our true identity. Usually we seek this identity in other places and according to other terms; we seek it in what we have done, and in what we own, and in what we hope to achieve. To look for it elsewhere does not mean that we seek to strip ourselves of all that is earthly or creaturely, but it does mean that we seek to attach ourselves to Christ. In this way our distinctiveness assumes a new form and shape. All our qualities, our talents, our earthly makeup, become part of the life we live as Christians, a life guided and permeated by the divine love which nourishes us at the very center.

PART THREE

OUR BEHAVIOR

It is to the prodigals — to those who exhaust all their strength in pursuing what seems to them good and who, after their strength has failed, go on impotently desiring — that the memory of their Father's house comes back. If the son had lived economically he would never have thought of returning.

Simone Weil, *Notebooks*

CHAPTER SIX

ETHICS AND FORGIVENESS

Divine love is active. God is at work in human beings, reshaping what is earthly by the power of his love, and we who bear his love are to be active as well. We are to love our neighbors. Immediately this raises a serious question. We are commanded to love, yet love cannot be commanded. We fall in love, in the case of romantic love; in the case of friendship or affection, we find ourselves simply liking a person. Since these feelings are not fully under our control, how is it that we can be "commanded" to have them?

This is the wrong way to approach the question. It is true that love cannot be commanded if love is only a feeling, but the very fact that we are commanded to love shows that love is not to be identified with feelings. To love is first and foremost to be *active,* rather than to feel. This is why Kierkegaard entitled one of his greatest books *Works of Love,* in order to stress that divine love, unlike human love, consists primarily of actions to be performed. It is not to act without feeling, for to act from divine love is also to care, and to care profoundly. It is, as we saw in the case of de Beausobre, to suffer cruel treatment and yet show kindness, in the hope that the evil of another can be lessened by our resistance to hatred or despair. It is to seek to understand the other, to release the other from debt. Our emotions, our sentiments, are involved in all these actions, but both the acts of love and the corresponding sentiments are far beyond the range of our natural endowment. Christian love involves both feelings and actions which are beyond our earthly power. Only the power of grace can overcome our inclination to care only for those we are attracted to, or for those human problems and needs we find interesting.

It is important to recall that Jesus' parable of the Good Samaritan is used in Luke's gospel to show what it is to be such a neighbor. The Levite and the priest pass by the stricken man on the road to Jericho, who was rendered so anonymous by brutality that he was just a piece of helpless and battered flesh. They were not necessarily "bad" men to pass by; there are needs, after all, to which spontaneous pity does not easily respond. If we are to meet them we will have first to overcome our initial revulsion. And as Simone Weil notes in a different context, "We have become so flabby that nowadays we think pity is something easy and hardness something difficult and meritorious."[24] This is how we are to understand the action, perverse at first sight, of St. Francis when he kissed the leper, kissed his very sores. Through the power of divine grace the saint showed those outside human society, those who had ceased to count as people anymore, that he cared. He showed this by embracing those who were untouchable, and indeed kissed the very places of their hideousness. So too the Good Samaritan restored a battered hulk of flesh by treating it as a fellow creature.

The power to act beyond our own temperament, training, native strength, and sympathy comes from the presence of divine love at the center of our being. It guides and directs us; it checks our natural tendencies; it strengthens our insufficiencies. Therefore God can *command* us to love because he can also enable us by his grace to act as he commands. As Kierkegaard points out in *Works of Love,* the fact that love of neighbor is couched in the form of a commandment shows us that this love is beyond our natural endowment, while it also shows us that we can seek to obey it when fed and nourished by a secret presence at our core.

But how does one establish such a claim? Whatever happens, one can always say that those who show great love for others by their sacrifices are simply acting from their own strength. People simply vary in their native endowment, training, and the effort they are willing to make, so how can we attribute their acts of love to God's grace at work in them?

In trying to illustrate what it means to live by the inspiration and activity of divine love, I would like to consider a very familiar story — the parable of the Prodigal Son in Luke's gospel. The story of a younger son's debauchery and an elder son's self-righteousness may seem a curious one to choose under the circumstances, and one which could only make the point by negation. But I hope in examining this story to uncover still another route to divine love, albeit an ambiguous one. That is the ethical route, with all its temptations and pitfalls, as well as the insights it reveals into our own behavior.

Because of its very familiarity a great deal of the force of this parable may be lost on us, so I would like to bring to bear on it some ideas Kierkegaard developed in another context. In several works, including *Either/Or,* Kierkegaard presents what he calls the "aesthetic life." By "aesthetics" he does not mean a life dedicated to the pursuit and appreciation of beauty, but rather a life lived on the basis of native endowments, or characteristics — a good mind, a good voice, or any other natural talent. One of the chief characteristics of the aesthetic life is its lack of continuity. The aesthetic life is made up of isolated episodes collected like beads on a string. Such a life is interesting only for its random episodes or experiences, just as the beads are what give a piece of string whatever interest it may have.

The aesthete judges everything, including other people, on the basis of their being "interesting." They either interest him or they don't; the world is divided up into these two categories, for the aesthete desires above all to be entertained. He cares only about the unusual and the extraordinary, in his desire to be fascinated, thrilled, and captivated. For boredom and the craving for novelty is not an accidental feature of the aesthetic life, but built into its very foundations. If we seek only gratification, and are guided in this search only by temperament and native endowment, we are bound to get bored. It becomes harder and harder to recapture the fascination and excitement of having done something for the first time, when so many things have been tried that there is nothing new to try. Chronic boredom is bad enough, but it is only the shadow of something worse. It is the shadow of real despair, the despair of a life which lacks validity.

In *Either/Or* Kierkegaard contrasts the aesthetic life to what he calls the ethical life, where the value of life does not depend on episode after episode, or novelty after novelty. An ethical person is guided by obligations. Such a life has significance through the fulfillment of obligations, for to the ethical person the world does not consist merely of the "interesting" and the "uninteresting." It consists of what is good, right, and precious, and what is evil, dishonorable, and despicable. The world is full of drama because good and evil are in conflict, and so our actions in such a universe partake of the same significance. It is a life that holds together and has continuity because it is guided by one overarching principle: obligation. It is also a life that grows in value at every moment of time; each additional moment of loyalty to obligations is an increment to this achievement.

I have chosen the parable of the Prodigal Son because it serves in part to expose the pitfalls of both the aesthetic and the ethical life, through Luke's portrayal of the younger and elder sons. We have, then, the story of one man who leaves his father's house to squander his fortune, and another who remains to fulfill his obligations: "There was a man who had two sons; and the younger of them said to his father, 'Father, give me the share of the property that falls to me.' And he divided his living between them. Not many days later, the younger son gathered all he had and took his journey into a far country, and there he squandered his property in loose living" (Lk. 15:11-13).

One way of looking at this younger son is in the character of Kierkegaard's aesthete, one whose life is dominated by a desire for immediate and varied gratifications. The son demands his inheritance to live his own way, according to his own lights, apart from all obligations to the giver — the father who gives him his freedom. But in time the bottom drops out of this life, for the son is not "lucky" enough to have the means to go on living riotously until he reaches the point of despair: "And when he had spent everything, a great famine arose in that country, and he began to be in want" (v. 14). The exhaustion of his resources, his self-sufficiency, and his hope forces the son to give up his way of life. This could be seen as a variation on the theme of the way of desire I spoke of much earlier, a metaphor for the void or emptiness at the center of each one of us that becomes exposed and remains exposed. In this case the exposure is involuntary; the younger son loses all he possesses, and is forced to go on desiring nonetheless.

Looking after someone else's swine makes him realize that he would be better off at home, for there even the hired hands have something to eat. So he decides to return to his father and confess his fault: "I will arise and go to my father, and I will say to him, 'Father, I have sinned against heaven and before you; I am no longer worthy to be called your son; treat me as one of your hired servants' " (vv. 18–19).

We cannot tell if the words, which literally taken are words of repentance, are in earnest. Does the son really recognize his obligations to his father, and see that life is not to be lived in doing only what interests and excites? Does he really renounce such a life? For the son is driven to return home out of desperation and exhaustion, with no viable alternative; it is a sense of futility that drives him. So the mere decision to go home and say these words does not necessarily show that he repented. The only possession remaining to him is his status as a son — his last card, so to speak. He plans out of desperation to relinquish his status as a son, in hopes that he might be treated as a hired servant at the very least.

There are, however, indications that the son is in earnest when he actually speaks to his father, the father who, when he first saw his son returning home, "had compassion, and ran and embraced and kissed him" (v. 20). With such a loving reception, the son was not actually forced to play his last card; he was already safe. But he did. What could have prompted such an act, but his father's behavior?

The father responds to a wayward son's return graciously. He does not meet him with the rebuke he deserves, nor ask for any bargains to be made in exchange for a lowly place in the household. He runs out to meet his son before any plea can be made. Such a gracious love has power over evil, the power to reduce it to nothing, so it is no longer there to motivate an action. This might be why the prodigal son, in the presence of such a gracious reception, can give up his last card by proceeding to say to his father the words he had planned, instead of keeping them to himself. Seeing he is safe, he does not for that reason hang on-to what he now does not have to relinquish: his status as a son. He does not clutch at his last card, but instead re-linquishes it voluntarily and confesses his fault. His desire and hunger are fed by a gracious presence, a loving and forgiving presence. So the prodigal son is free to act as he does, in repenting of his effort to find fullness of life in his own way. His father gives orders that he is to be clothed in the best robe, and given a ring and sandals, and that a ban-quet is to be prepared. He who was dead is pronounced alive — brought to life through a father's love, and able to live from this love.

The younger son's repentance arises from his exhaus-tion and his desire, but what of the elder son? Luke tells us, "he was angry and refused to go in. His father came out and entreated him, but he answered his father, 'Lo, these many years I have served you, and I never disobeyed your command . . .' " (vv. 28–29). The elder son is furious when he learns of his father's reception of the wastrel younger brother for the very reason that he himself has been responsible all his life, held himself accountable, and met his obligations. In short, he lives ethically, and we can see in him the very real dangers of the ethical life. Precisely because the elder son is aware of his obligations and meets them, he cannot recognize in his father's behavior an act of love. He can neither rejoice over his brother's repentance nor, finally, can he know what it is to live from his father's love.

One pitfall of the ethical life is our confidence in the fact that our obligations can be met. This confidence can come about simply because our standards are not particu-larly high, but it tends to occur more because through ac-quired self-discipline we are able to live an orderly life and make our contribution to society. In either case we are sin-cere individuals, our consciences are clear, and our confidence is secure. When that confidence begins to ebb, however, the more we become aware of the vastness of our obligations and the mixed nature of our motives. We become increasingly sensitive to failure, as well as to the impossibility of achieving perfection. The more good deeds we perform, the more we can become oppressed by the magnitude of the deeds undone and the deeds impossible to do. We may well lead significant and moral lives, believing that good and evil are real and that some things are to be fought for, sacrificed and even died for, yet in that very commitment to obligation we may come to the point of despair. We may come to feel, as St. Paul did, that "I can will what is right, but I cannot do it. For I do not do the good I want, but the evil I do not want is what I do" (Rom. 7:18–19). Dismay can weigh more and more heavily on us until we start to doubt the validity of our own life, and even to despair of ourselves.

Another pitfall of the ethical life is simple weariness. In St. Paul's letter to the church in Galatia he cautions the Christians there, "And let us not grow weary in well-doing, for in due season we shall reap, if we do not lose heart" (Gal. 6:9). It is easy to weary of trying to do what is right when others do not, when all around us we see people cutting corners, or living shabby and frivolous lives.

Clearly the elder son in this parable has confidence in his own ability to meet his obligations, and that is one reason why the basis of his relationship to his father is not that of living from and by his father's love. Had it been so, he would not have felt he had a grievance against his father for his graciousness toward the prodigal. For the elder son would have recognized that the prodigal's relationship to the father is grounded solely in a father's generous love, just as is his own. He does not see this precisely because his own relationship to his father is based on his own strength in meeting his obligations. Had he reached the point of dismay, been reduced to despair because of his obligations, the son might have been driven to his father's love — just as his brother was driven by exhaustion and hunger. As it is, the son stands with confidence before his father, and declares his own obedience with a deep sense of grievance against his father's generosity. Because he lives from his own achievement and not from this generosity, he cannot believe it when his father says to him, "Son, you are always with me, and all that is mine is yours" (v. 31).

In *The Four Loves* C.S. Lewis captures very well the difficulty of learning that we are well-pleasing to God because of the fact that we receive his love, and not because of our achievements and talents.

> All those expressions of unworthiness which Christian practice puts into the believer's mouth seem to the outer world like the degraded and insincere grovellings of a sycophant before a tyrant, or at best a *façon de parler* like the self-depreciation of a Chinese gentleman when he calls himself "this coarse and illiterate person." In reality, however, they express the continually renewed, because continually necessary, attempt to negate that misconception of ourselves and of our relation to God which nature, even while we pray, is always recommending to us. No sooner do we believe that God loves us than there is an impulse to believe that He does so, not because He is Love, but because we are intrinsically lovable. The Pagans obeyed this impulse unabashed; a good man was "dear to the gods" because he was good. We, being better taught, resort to subterfuge. Far be it from us to think that we have virtues for which God could love us. But then, how magnificently we have repented! As Bunyan says, describing his first and illusory conversion, "I thought there was no man in England that pleased God better than I." Beaten out of this, we next offer our own humility to God's admiration. Surely He'll like *that*? Or if not that, our clear-sighted and humble recognition that we still lack humility. Thus, depth beneath depth and subtlety within subtlety, there remains some lingering idea of our own, our very own, attractiveness. It is easy to acknowledge, but almost impossible to realise for long, that we are mirrors whose brightness, if we are bright, is wholly derived from the sun that shines upon us. Surely we must have a little — however little — native luminosity? Surely we can't be *quite* creatures?[25]

As long as we rely on our own strength and natural endowments we do not live from a Father's love. Confidence in our ability to meet our obligations can thus be as dangerous as waste and prodigality. Both sons have a void, an emptiness at the center of their person, which is to be fed by a father's graciousness. To follow the way of desire, as the prodigal does, may lead to a life that is forever like that of a leaky vessel, unless we voluntarily expose that emptiness. Or circumstances may be such that we run out of resources, and thus find our void *forcefully* exposed. In either case, the route of desire involves suffering.

It is not "wrong" for us to fulfill all our obligations so far as we are aware of them, as the prodigal's elder brother does. The danger of "well-doing" is that it may blind us to the fact that we are creatures dependent on a Father's graciousness. All that we are, all our natural endowments, is given to us by the Father's creative love, and we are pleasing to him simply in our recognition of this.

Rather than a barrier, the ethical route can instead be a route to God, but only when our confidence in our ability to meet our obligations is broken. We need not be driven to the point of utter dismay or despair, but merely to have grown weary of well-doing, in order to break through the barrier that keeps us from a Father's love as the basis of our activity. I believe that many responsible people, including many church people, are weary of obligations. They feel pushed and pulled from every side by obligations that never seem to end, by the burden of these obligations and by guilt at the fact that they resent them. That guilt may drive them to try harder, but the load is heavy and to carry it seems more and more futile all the time.

It is just at this point of weariness that we can become open to the graciousness of God, and our soul can open to Jesus' words, "Come to me, all who labor and are heavy laden, and I will give you rest" (Matt. 11:28). We can then cease to be weary — not because we have thrown off our obligations, but because we are being carried and strengthened by the Father's love that has now found access. As long as our confidence remains intact, our success at meeting obligations remains a barrier to living from divine love. We cannot understand its graciousness to others and we can even become angry and bitter at the forgiveness shown to "worthless" people by others, as was the elder son.

For is it not immoral to let people off for failure to do what they could have done, but did not? Immanuel Kant, the great eighteenth century philosopher, thought so, and in the book *Religion Within the Limits of Reason Alone* he argues that a person is to be forgiven only if he deserves it. God therefore cannot graciously forgive a person. In this Kant ignores the fact that a Father's love must *precede* all moral obligations. We exist only because a Father's love graciously creates us, and his desire is that we be related to him by love. God's forgiveness is to reconnect us in our inmost being to his love, and only his graciousness can do it. For how can the prodigal son, who indeed could have been a dutiful son but was not, ever become his father's son in honor? Since he has dishonored his father by turning to disorderly living, even the prodigal's repentence and confession of sin cannot restore him to his place of innocence and honor. Obligation to a father is not an abstract moral law, for it demands a personal response toward the one to whom one is obligated. This father was violated by the prodigal's refusal to accept the tasks which go with being a son.

Only a father's love that can treat a son as one who owes him nothing can restore the son to honor. Such a love only asks to be received, only asks to be lived by, only asks to be consumed as food.

This is captured in a poem by George Herbert.

Love bade me welcome; yet my soul drew back,
  Guiltie of dust and sinne.
But quick-ey'd Love, observing me grow slack
  From my first entrance in,
Drew nearer to me, sweetly questioning
  If I lack'd anything.

'A guest,' I answer'd, 'worthy to be here':
  Love said, 'You shall be he.'
'I, the unkind, ungrateful? Ah, my dear,
  I cannot look on Thee.'
Love took my hand, and smiling did reply,
  'Who made the eyes but I?'

'Truth, Lord; but I have marr'd them; let my shame
  Go where it doth deserve.'
'And know you not,' says Love, 'Who bore the blame?'
  'My dear, then I will serve.'
'You must sit down,' says Love, 'and taste My meat.'
  So I did sit and eat.26

The last line is very simple, almost laughably so. Love bids the poet sit and eat, and he does. There is the same simplicity in the father's banquet for the son returning hungry, and in the honor of a ring upon his finger, the best robe, and shoes upon his feet. To live by our Father's love is to know our own poverty — either in the midst of famine, as the prodigal did, or in the midst of plenty. It is this knowledge and this hunger which must precede ethics, and all strivings to lead the ethical life. We can be without any shame at our knowledge of this poverty, for such shame is lost in our rejoicing over the Father's bounty.

CHAPTER SEVEN

HUMAN NEED AND CHRISTIAN ACTION

Learning to live from divine love immediately brings up the question of activity, the activity to which we who bear the love of Christ are called. This activity is very ordinary and mundane indeed, for it has to do with our response to the day-to-day needs of our neighbors; the question it raises, however, is far from ordinary. What *do* people need? For once we go beyond the most obvious needs for food, clothing, and shelter, we realize there have always been disagreements about what it means to live a fully human life. To supply just one instance of this, Werner Jaeger's monumental three-volume study of Hellenic culture, *Paideia,* traces the different ideas of human excellence in Greek life and thought. In Homer's time, for example, the height of excellence was to be "a doer of deeds and a sayer of words." This attitude reflects the ideal of the aristocracy, whose time was spent in training for war. Excellence was measured by individual deeds of valor and the ability to speak well in councils of war, where eloquence was another form of prowess and one more way of displaying individual merit.

Much of the ancient world's philosophy was concerned with the nature of human happiness, and how it was to be achieved. The wide spectrum of opinion included the Epicurean stress on pleasure, the Stoic stress on invulnerability and independence, and the Aristotelian claim for intellectual contemplation. In our society this feature of philosophy is performed by psychology, especially of the popular sort, and there is one aspect of the ancient world's discussion of happiness, or what we would call "fulfillment," directly relevant to us. In Plato's dialogue the *Phaedrus* there is a speech on sexual gratification, supposedly written by a famous Sophist named Lysias. A Sophist was a teacher of *areté,* nowadays translated as "virtue," which really means "human excellence." A Sophist was supposed to be an expert on how to attain human excellence or fulfillment; in practice, it meant an expert on the successful gratification of desires.

In his speech Lysias argues that to succeed in one's desire for sexual gratification, it is better not to be in love. He claims that to be in love is to lack self-control, for the lover is moved to do many foolish things — such as give extravagant gifts, neglect business and practical affairs, and suffer from jealousy. Should the lover fall out of love he is bound to regret all the gifts he has given, as well as be faced with the trouble of getting rid of the beloved. So Lysias argues that sexual pleasure between people who are not in love is far better than sexual pleasure between lovers, a harmless way of pursuing the gratification of desire.

Lysias' argument in the *Phaedrus* raises a much larger question, for it raises an important issue for us concerning *all* our desires. Namely, how are we to judge the proper way for our desires to be fulfilled? We are a mass of desires that ask for gratification, just as our bodies ask for food. The Sophist is an expert on the successful or efficient "feeding" of desires. The parallel nowadays, as I have said, is popular and not so popular psychologies that tell us how to satisfy our needs with a view to living more satisfactory lives. It is often said that our basic needs cannot be denied without great harm, and we must learn how to untangle and understand our conflicting desires so as to attain an integrated personality. The question I want to ask is, can there be a science or a knowledge of the ways in which our desires ought to be gratified, such as ancient Sophists claimed and modern psychologists are sometimes thought to suggest? Is it possible to achieve the knowledge of what people need through a study of their desires, and nothing else? Can our desires provide enought data to tell us what we should seek, or how we should go about seeking it?

Let me start by contrasting human desires to bodily needs. The body needs food, there are many foods which can feed the body, and not every food is equally good. How food tastes is certainly not an adequate guide to its nutritional value. We can determine nutritional value fairly accurately by studying the effects of various foods on the body. The key question is — can we do the same with the things we use to satisfy our desires? Lysias tries to do so with sexual desire, by showing the unfortunate consequences of love and the advantages of sexual pleasure without love. For him, the pluses and minuses of gaining sexual gratification without love outweigh those of sexual gratification with love.

Socrates in the *Phaedrus* gives a speech which parallels that of Lysias, and claims that Lysias has made a mistake in his calculation. But after giving this speech Socrates is revolted; he is ashamed of this way of discussing love. To find out how a human being ought to live cannot be determined merely by consulting desires, and then calculating how successfully or unsuccessfully they are gratified by the pursuit of one course of action instead of another. We can determine what to eat and how much to eat because the condition of bodily health is the natural state of a body, as well as the goal nature establishes for the body. But what is the goal or purpose of human life? This question cannot be answered by looking only at the body or only at human desires and at what gratifies them, for it may be the case that attainment of a maximum of gratification is not the purpose of human life.

As Socrates points out, it may be that our destiny lies in establishing contact with a nonearthly reality, and this is what he understands by the famous inscription at Delphi, "Know thyself." To know oneself is to know what is true about human beings. Is their destiny an earthly one, or is it to be found in contact with a reality which transcends the earth? We cannot find out the answer by a study of human desires alone, since all these desires are for earthly things. It will not bring us any closer to learning the primary truth about ourselves; desires for what is earthly cannot reveal to us the truth of what we are.

The Sophists ignored this primary issue, pretending that study of these desires was an efficient way to find human fulfillment. I expect they knew quite a lot about successful gratification, just as we today have learned even more by our knowledge of unconscious psychic conflicts, and the use of psychological therapies leading to a more satisfying attainment of what we want. To exclude every consideration but our earthly desires, however, is to be un-scientific in the fundamental sense of that term. It is to shut off a possibility arbitrarily and to lack, from within the restricted data examined, a sufficient basis for any judgment concerning a vitally relevant matter. That Plato, speaking through the mouth of Socrates, could see this fact with such clarity and expect it to be visible to any reflective person, without the aid of Christian revelation, is indicative.

The truth about the limited nature of human desires is frequently attested to in the parables and teachings of Jesus. In his journey with his disciples through the villages of Caesarea Philippi, Jesus says to his disciples, "For what does it profit a man, to gain the whole world and forfeit his life? For what can a man give in return for his life?'' (Mk. 8:36–37). There is no profit for us in all that we can gain and achieve, if what we require for a vital part of our life is lacking. We strive after all sorts of things, but if we achieved them all what would it profit us? We would not gain what could fill and satisfy us, while losing the chance to receive what would. In Luke's parable of the Rich Fool the rich man says to himself, "I will pull down my barns, and build larger ones; and there I will store all my grain and my goods. And I will say to my soul, Soul, you have ample goods laid up for many years; take your ease, eat, drink, be merry" (Lk. 12:18–19). The man is not wicked, or selfish, or evil — he is merely a fool, which is why the last line of this parable so rivets our attention: "Fool! This night your soul is required of you; and the things you have prepared, whose will they be?" (v. 20). We cannot discover what might give us fulfillment by consulting our desires alone, as the rich fool does, as long as there is a possibility that we have a destiny beyond these desires.

Ancient sophistry, modern psychology, and any teaching which promises earthly happiness have enormous appeal. Sometimes these correctly teach us about the connection between our desires and their satisfaction, and may indeed enable us to fulfill our ambitions. But this does not, and cannot, address itself to the simple but crucial question of what we are. Are we creatures of the earth, destined to live from the earth only, or are we also called to know and live from a divine love? One of the costs of making our desires the only data, and success in the pursuit of their gratification our only goal, is blindness.

For the divine love at work within us to be directed intelligently, therefore, we must focus not on our desires but on our needs. We have intimations of needs beyond those satisfied by food and shelter, or achievement and reputation; in addition to these bodily and earthly needs, we have what Simone Weil calls the heavenly needs of our soul. It is only in distinguishing these three kinds of need and the ways in which they can be met that we can specify the distinctive goal, motive, and manner of Christian action.

We have a "heavenly" need because there is a hunger for something that nothing in this world can assuage, but we have other needs which are not met directly by God's presence. We have "earthly" needs, as distinct from bodily needs, and among these I include the need for friendship, respect, achievement, and responsibility. When such needs go unmet, we cannot develop properly as creatures. These needs, extremely numerous and varied, are not bodily needs; following Simone Weil's usage, I call them the "earthly needs of the soul." These three types of need are obviously connected. To put it simply, there are clothes and clothes, shelters and shelters. The way in which provision is made for our bodily needs can actually minister to earthly needs — such as the need for respect — and even to the heavenly needs of the soul.

It may be merely a commonplace to say that the needs of the body as well as the earthly needs of the soul can be neglected to such a degree that people are reduced to a state of desperation. They lack food, clothing, and shelter, or they live in restricted and brutalizing conditions, as do migrant farm workers in rural areas and dwellers in urban ghettos. They are caught up in and trapped by crippling political, social, and economic forces. Although these are "earthly" conditions, it should be apparent from what I have said about the cross that concern for people in desperate situations is at the core of loving Jesus Christ. Not to care for those who are severely deprived is to lack the capacity to love him who, on the cross, was deprived as well. To turn from people made desperate by such unmet needs is to be blind to the cross of Christ. In the parable of the sheep and the goats Jesus explicitly identifies himself with those in desperate need, so that if we love him we cannot help but turn to them as well:

> Come, O blessed of my Father, inherit the kingdom prepared for you from the foundation of the world; for I was hungry and you gave me food, I was thirsty and you gave me drink, I was a stranger and you welcomed me, I was naked and you clothed me, I was sick and you visited me, I was in prison and you came to me. (Matt. 25:34–36)

Concern for those in severe need is not a matter of choice for a Christian; it is to be a Christian.

We are also to concern ourselves with the physical needs of people and the social conditions which brutalize them, because such conditions deprive them of the opportunity to open themselves to God's love. The beauty of the world does not seem to reach the brutalized products of an urban hell: they do not acquire it through their senses, and their intellect is not directed to that end through study of the laws of the universe. Nor is the love of God as found through the route of desire likely to reach people seriously deprived. The more fortunate have the opportunity to learn that no matter how much they acquire and achieve, it is never enough to satisfy them. By contrast, the consciousness of the poor is taken up with what they do *not* possess, what they cannot achieve, so how can they ever come to recognize the one need that such things can never fill? The poor cannot experience the emptiness only God can feed, because of the pain caused by a multitude of empty spaces within themselves.

Even the sufferings that the poor undergo, either from the accidents of nature or from human cruelty, do not necessarily open them to a knowledge of divine love. They have not come to know God by other means, so there remains only the experience of the single force of gravity — gravity in all its crudeness. To suffer brutal conditions deprives such people of their one vital freedom — the ability to yield themselves to the love of God.

We often become so overwhelmed by the massiveness and complexity of social, political, and economic evils that we are paralyzed into inaction. Consider, on the other hand, the work of Mother Teresa of Calcutta, who does not have the power to change these conditions either. Part of her work is to take care of the destitute and dying, work she does out of a distinctive kind of compassion. It is a compassion that enables them to know something beyond the crushing force of circumstance.

> We want them to know that there are people who really love them, who really want them, at least for the few hours they have to live, to know human and divine love. That they too may know that they are children of God, and that they are not forgotten and that they are loved and cared about and that there are young lives ready to give themselves in their service.27

This is the *distinctive* nature of Christian action, action that meets human affliction with reverence. It is meeting a sufferer's bodily needs in a manner which also satisfies the heavenly needs of the soul. This graciousness awakens in its recipient a capacity for saying "yes" or "no" to a gracious presence. To treat the afflicted with reverence offers them the opportunity to love God even though they may not know it is God they love.

Mother Teresa's reverence for the lives of the poor is based on her assumption that their response matters, and that they have not lost the integrity of this response. In society's eyes the destitute and dying may have forfeited this right, yet she treats them as people created to know and respond to God's love, and in this way to be worthy of respect. Mother Teresa can show this reverence because she operates from the energy supplied by grace, rather than from the energy arising solely from her own human attributes: "If we did not see Jesus in what we touch, we couldn't do it. Some of the work is quite repulsive."[28]

So the manner in which we respond is crucial. Unless the love of God lies at the root of our activity, we will not care for the afflicted or destitute in a way that preserves or restores their one vital freedom. Instead, we will enslave them even further by our "charity."

If the poor are truly powerless, they may be taken into account merely out of pity. Such pity is precarious, however, for it depends only on human whim or caprice. Many church and secular appeals for aid show pictures of "pitiful" people, true enough, but some people in need are too ugly to make us feel pity. Instead, they evoke disgust. So much of charity is simply the result of the balance of gravity in the makeup of our personality. We give where we *feel* pity; we do not give when we don't, and we do not give out of a sense of solidarity. This sense of solidarity with all human affliction or lack can only arise with the recognition that all of us are equally subject to the laws of nature. These can reduce any one of us to anonymity at any time, regardless of our merits or demerits or social position. And our social condition is vulnerable to the onset of rapid inflation, or the closure of a government installation in our town, or the sudden death of a breadwinner. Circumstances often make or break us through no fault of our own; we are all vulnerable, and our lives are all precarious. Pity, accompanied by a sense of reverence, can arise from such a sense of solidarity. We can recognize in another's misery the unavoidable possibility of our own, and so are not separated from this misery by an impassible gulf.

Social action that disregards the heavenly needs of the soul as a crucial ingredient in social action itself is inadequate. There is a distinctively Christian reason, goal, and manner of action which recognizes at least three distinct but interconnected kinds of need. Social action without the humility caused by the recognition of heavenly need differs only in *degree,* not in kind, from injustice. The fact that social action and injustice differ only in degree is significant; though they both belong to the earthly realm, some good is accomplished by, let us say, the reform of judicial procedures, slum clearance, and educational opportunities. But Mother Teresa reminds us,

> It is not very often *things* [italics mine] they need. What they need much more is what we offer them. In these twenty years of work amongst the people, I have come more and more to realize that it is being unwanted that is the worst disease that any human being can ever experience.[29]

Another implicit danger in undertaking social causes without humility lies in the fact that such social action must constantly replenish its energies, its good intentions, in the struggle for social justice. It is useful to remember here Simone Weil's analogy of a family caring for its invalid member, where a diminished supply of energy "fuels" itself on resentment and self-pity as well as on love. In this sphere, two sources of supply are the twin vices of self-righteousness toward those indifferent to social action, or merely slack, and hatred for those who actively oppose it. Besides, it is simply beyond our human powers to act without a sense of superiority toward those we help; seen through the eyes of our "gravity," such people are indeed inferior. This attitude will bear evil fruit in the life of the giver, if nowhere else.

In addition to a Christian concern for people's bodily and earthly needs, there is the direct provision for people's heavenly need through teaching, preaching, and the sacraments. Through these God feeds our hunger for what is not of this world. But the attempt to convey divine love to others in this way, to people whose earthly condition is unpleasant or grim, must also be made with respect and reverence. How can anyone preach the love of God without taking care that the hearers know God's love in all its fullness? To know it in all its fullness is to receive it through the beauty of the world, and through the pleasant side of creation. The love of God must be experienced through the senses, the intellect, and the social order, and not shared only through the proclamation that Christ endured the cross for all our sakes.

Both a gospel that lacks social concern as a necessary ingredient, as well as a social concern that neglects the needs of the soul as a necessary element in social action, are inadequate. Neither conveys the breadth and depth of the divine love. It is misleading to say, "We must be concerned for the gospel *and* social action," for it is not a question of adding something onto the gospel. Only through its desire to alleviate other crushing burdens can preaching amount to a genuine desire for people to know God's love. Otherwise, such proclamation is not a gracious act. It may do some good, just as social action without recognition of people's heavenly need may do some good. But such an approach serves, in the end, merely to trivialize the gospel. It trivializes the very nature of love and service, because it fails to recognize the depth and variety of human need. At the very least it brings shame to Christ's name, for this attitude assumes that God's love is limited, and does not extend to every sphere of human life.

CHAPTER EIGHT

CHRISTIAN WORSHIP

In the earlier chapters of this book I used the analogy of intersecting planes in geometry to describe the way in which God crosses the human plane. Throughout, I have tried to show the various "points" at which we can sense God's life intersecting our own, points which include experiences of suffering, grief, and physical hardship. I have dwelt on these experiences largely because such evils can be major stumbling-blocks to our faith and to our awareness of God's presence, and I am well aware of the impediments these experiences impose. In extending this metaphor of intersecting planes to include the church as one more point where the two realms intersect, the human and the divine, I am bringing up difficulties of quite a different order. The practice of Christian worship and the ordeals of human suffering are worlds apart, yet it is often difficult to translate the insights gained by the latter into the practice of the former. It is hard to transpose the insights of extreme situations into a situation that is very ordinary for most of us — the mundane, day-to-day ritual of engaging in Christian worship.

The very fact that worship takes place at all is enough to show that Christianity can never be reduced to mere ideas. We do use ideas, and they are essential to the forging of a commitment to God and to the act of worship, but all our thought and study finds its culmination in worship of the divine reality. In this act of yielding our entire nature to divine love, the earthly and the divine realms meet, intersect, and become one. Human beings become a heavenly society, existing in this world but not of it because of the presence of another reality in their midst, a reality that unites them to itself and one another. This reality dwells in the center of each person. Worship is a time and a place where human beings rejoice at receiving heavenly food, and rejoice in the bond of love thus created between them.

What I describe is an ideal of worship; the reality can be just the opposite. Our minds wander from the liturgy and we can't listen to the sermon. The church service itself becomes so familiar that there is a tendency to take it for granted and go on to other things — programs of social action, of counselling, of choirs and music, of adult education — with worship becoming rather low on our scale of priorities. And when we do assign a high value to liturgical practice, we tend to assign too much. At those times we try to make the worship more "interesting," and this is too often done in the spirit of Kierkegaard's aesthete, who always wants some novelty to keep boredom at bay. If the focus is on making the service interesting, this becomes the basis for determining what is to be done and why it is to be done. The fact that the purpose of worship is "to ascribe worth" to another, the Anglo-Saxon meaning of the word *woerthscripe,* disappears.

What we must renounce even when at church is an illusion, the illusion that by all this activity we can find the one who alone feeds our hunger for life. It is painful to renounce an illusion: for it is what keeps us going, keeps us hustling, keeps us busy, keeps us hopeful. To lose this illusion is a kind of death, the kind of death Jesus told his disciples we must all undergo: "Whoever seeks to gain his life will lose it, but whoever loses his life will preserve it" (Lk. 17:33). There is an emptiness at our core that is like a Black Hole in space. A Black Hole sucks down all matter, and there is an emptiness in us which threatens to suck us down as well, although what it is actually doing is dispelling an illusion. It is not destroying us, but revealing to us that we are already a dead thing trying to give itself life by taking in all within its reach. But the core of us remains an emptiness. To be a person, a soul, is to need something beyond oneself to live; whatever we can *grasp* cannot give us life. No matter what efforts we make to fill ourselves, we always find ourselves once again empty. We carry that emptiness and that deadness within us, for it is the annihilation that Donne describes in his *Devotions*:

> This is *Natures nest of Boxes;* The *Heavens* containe the *Earth,* the *Earth, Cities, Cities, Men.* And all these are *Concentrique;* the common *center* to them all, is *decay, ruine;* only . . . That light, which is the very emanation of the light of *God,* in which the *Saints* shall dwell, with which the *Saints* shall be appareld, only . . . that which was not made of *Nothing,* is not threatned with this annihilation. All other things are; even *Angels,* even our *soules;* they move upon the same *poles,* they bend to the same *Center;* and if they were not made immortall by *preservation,* their *Nature* could not keepe them from sinking to this *center, Annihilation.*

Yet time and again, without our always being clear why it happens, we find that Jesus' words hold us. We find ourselves hearing once again, perhaps for the hundredth time, something which Jesus did or said that fills and nourishes us. The institutional church has to be a place where this possibility may be actualized again and again. This is merely one way of saying that the primary function of the institutional church is worship. Christ is heavenly food. Those who hunger for what the world cannot provide and have tasted of him know the uniqueness of the hunger and the uniqueness of the food.

There is no question about the huge variety of human needs which heavenly food does not directly nourish, for we need air, meat and drink, shelter, and friendship.

Prayer and praise do not directly supply these needs. If we have to argue, on the other hand, as to whether there is a hunger that is met and only met by the food of Christ, then the degree of our uncertainty is a precise measure of the degree of our idolatry. For whatever our lips may *say* about God, church, and Christianity, we do not worship God. We do not live from his nourishment at the core of our being; we have not yielded ourselves to divine love, but are seeking life elsewhere.

When Simon Peter met the risen Lord by the shore of a lake, the Lord he had betrayed, Jesus asked him, "Simon, son of John, do you love me?" Just as Peter denied him three times, Jesus asked this of Peter three times. Each time Peter answered that he did, Jesus' reply to him was the same: "Feed my sheep" (John 21:17). We betray Jesus in any and all of our church activity — programs, sermons, theologies, and ministries — that do not recognize that it is his words, his life, his Spirit, his body, and his blood that feed us.

A few years ago it was asked, "What is the church doing?" The question was rhetorical, as though it were obvious that the church was doing precious little to meet the needs of the world. It was a charge that hurt badly, not only because people's needs are immense and our efforts in comparison are small, but also because we in our ignorance did not really know what it was that we ought to be doing. We did not know well enough what the standards were by which we should measure our activity or inactivity. Part of what we ought to be doing is meeting the heavenly need of the soul, and it is hard to measure the church's efficacy by standards that are clearly of this world. Still, it has to be done, and much criticism of the church's failure is based upon an evaluation which is either ignorant of the heavenly need of the soul, or has allowed it to fall out of sight. To stress the importance of this need as a primary part of the church's work can be seen as a dodge from other tasks; at the same time, other tasks are often used to dodge this one. Peter was asked, "Do you love me?" We need to ask ourselves the same question.

If we do love, then we know that we also live from him. That life always involves a willingness to be exposed, and a refusal to distract ourselves from the wound we have within. It is as if we have been burned, and the skin around the wound is so tender that it hurts just to breathe on it. No wonder we ignore it with every comforting word we can muster, a multitude of words, true as well as false. Who can object to them, since so many of them are true? But true words can hide a greater truth, and hide it much more effectively than lies; lies are more easily exposed. But true words, words that analyze the human personality, or words that analyze society, or words that analyze exploitation, or words that analyze religion — all of these can cover over and hide a wound. But they cannot heal it, for the wound at our center can be healed only by Christ. Our suffering is the very place where he begins his rule, the place where he is to commence his kingdom by giving himself to us.

In Dostoyevsky's novel, *The Brothers Karamazov,* a father has quarrelled for years with his eldest son, Dimitri, over the family property and over a woman. The father is an utter sensualist and his personality is powerfully present in all three sons, most obviously in Dimitri. The eldest son and the father agree to accept the judgment of a holy monk on the disputed property but, when they go to him and present their case, the monk will not pronounce judgment. Instead, he reverently kneels and bows his forehead to the floor at Dimitri's feet. This reaction shocks the onlookers, to whom the spiritual discernment of the holy man is well known, while Dimitri has the reputation of a fighter and a drunkard. What could he mean by this gesture?

The monk is not deceived, for he knows only too well that the issues here go far deeper than the ownership of some property and the possession of a woman. He understands that the elder brother is destined to suffer greatly, for Dimitri is one of those souls powerfully drawn by the powers which lead to death, and yet will not surrender to them. The holy man bows reverently before such suffering, "ascribing worth" to it, and in this suffering he recognizes the redemptive way of Christ.

NOTES

NOTES

1. M. O'C. Drury, "Madness and Religion," *The Danger of Words* (London: Routledge & Kegan Paul, 1973), pp. 115–137.
2. Friedrich Dürrenmatt, "Nachtliches Gesprach mit einem Verachten Menschen," in *Gesammelte Horspiele* (Zurich: Peter Schifferli, 1960), pp. 93–111. The translation is my own.
3. Simone Weil, *Gravity and Grace,* trans. Emma Craufurd (London: Routledge & Kegan Paul, 1952), p. 1.
4. *Ibid.*
5. *Ibid.,* p. 2.
6. Ray Lindquist, "Common Life" (Austin, Texas: Cold Mountain Press, 1973). Reprinted by permission of the author.
7. See especially Sister Basilea Schlink, *The Blessings of Illness* (Carol Stream, Ill.: Creation House, 1977).
8. Edith Barfoot, *The Joyful Vocation to Suffering,* reprinted in *The Witness of Edith Barfoot* (Oxford: Basil Blackwell, 1977).
9. Simone Weil, *Waiting on God,* trans. Emma Craufurd (Glasgow: Collins, 1959), pp. 35–36.
10. See especially Simone Weil, "The Love of God and Affliction," in *On Science, Necessity, and the Love of God,* trans. Richard Rees (London: Oxford University Press, 1968). The idea of the Father and the Son as separated by a distance and yet united through love is also largely based upon this essay.

11. Iulia de Beausobre, *The Woman Who Could Not Die* (New York: Viking Press, 1938); *Creative Suffering* (Westminster: Dacre Press, 1940). For other examples of similar experiences see H. Gollwitzer *et al.,* eds., *Dying We Live,* trans. R. Kuhn (New York: Pantheon Books, 1956). This work is a collection of materials left by Germans who were imprisoned and finally executed for their resistance to the Nazis.
12. *The Woman,* pp. 10–11.
13. *Creative Suffering,* p. 38.
14. *Ibid.,* p. 39.
15. *The Woman,* p. 178; *ibid.; ibid.,* p. 77.
16. *Creative Suffering,* pp. 40–41.
17. *The Woman,* pp. 86–87.
18. *Ibid.,* p. 88.
19. *Creative Suffering,* pp. 42–43.
20. *The Woman,* pp. 165–166.
21. *Creative Suffering,* pp. 43–44.
22. *The Woman,* p. 89.
23. *Creative Suffering,* p. 41.
24. Simone Weil, *The Notebooks of Simone Weil,* trans. Arthur Wills, 2 vols. (London: Routledge & Kegan Paul, 1956).
25. C.S. Lewis, *The Four Loves* (London: Geoffrey Bles, 1960), pp. 148–149.
26. George Herbert, "Love," in *Poems of George Herbert* (London: Oxford University Press, 1907), pp. 195–196.
27. Malcolm Muggeridge, *Something Beautiful for God* (New York: Harper & Row, 1971), p. 92.
28. *The New York Times,* 6 April 1979.
29. Muggeridge, pp. 98–99.
30. John Donne, "Tenth Meditation," *Devotions Upon Emergent Occasions,* ed. Anthony Raspa (Montreal and London: McGill-Queens University Press, 1975), p. 51.